Digital Marketing Minimum

Paramendra Kumar Bhagat
www.paramendra.com

Table Of Contents

Foreword..4
1. Introduction To Digital Marketing..5
    1.1 What is Digital Marketing?..6
    1.2 Evolution of Digital Marketing...9
    1.3 Benefits of Digital Marketing..12
    1.4 Key Digital Marketing Terminologies.. 16
    1.5 Overview of Digital Marketing Channels...................................... 19
2. Website Optimization and Design.. 22
    2.1 Importance of Website Optimization.. 23
    2.2 User Experience (UX) Design Principles......................................27
    2.3 Responsive Web Design.. 30
    2.4 Website Navigation and Structure.. 33
    2.5 Conversion Rate Optimization (CRO).. 37
3. Search Engine Optimization (SEO).. 40
    3.1 Fundamentals of SEO.. 41
    3.2 Keyword Research and Analysis..44
    2.3 On-Page Optimization Techniques...47
    3.4 Off-Page Optimization Strategies... 51
    3.5 SEO Tools and Analytics... 55
4. Pay-Per-Click (PPC) Advertising.. 59
    4.1 Introduction to PPC Advertising... 60
    4.2 Google Ads (Formerly AdWords)... 64
    4.3 Bing Ads And Other PPC Platforms... 68
    4.4 Creating Effective PPC Campaigns... 72
    4.5 PPC Analytics and Optimization...76
5. Social Media Marketing.. 80
    5.1 Overview of Social Media Marketing.. 81
    5.2 Social Media Platforms and Their Audiences...............................85
    5.3 Creating Engaging Social Media Content.................................... 89
    5.4 Social Media Advertising.. 93
    5.5 Social Media Analytics and Reporting.. 97
6. Email Marketing...101
    6.1 Introduction to Email Marketing..102

    6.2 Building An Email List And Segmentation 106
    6.3 Designing Effective Email Campaigns 110
    6.4 Email Automation and Personalization 114
    6.5 Email Marketing Analytics 118

7. Content Marketing 122
    7.1 What is Content Marketing? 123
    7.2 Content Strategy and Planning 127
    7.3 Creating Compelling Content 131
    7.4 Content Distribution And Promotion 134
    7.5 Content Marketing Metrics And Measurement 138

8. Influencer Marketing 142
    8.1 Introduction To Influencer Marketing 143
    8.2 Identifying And Engaging With Influencers 147
    8.3 Negotiating and Managing Influencer Partnerships 151
    8.4 Measuring Influencer Marketing ROI 154
    8.5 Influencer Marketing Best Practices 158

9. Mobile Marketing 161
    9.1 Mobile Marketing Landscape 162
    9.2 Mobile Advertising Formats And Platforms 166
    9.3 App Store Optimization (ASO) 170
    9.4 SMS Marketing 174
    9.5 Mobile Marketing Analytics 178

10. Analytics and Reporting 182
    10.1 Introduction To Digital Marketing Analytics 183
    10.2 Setting Key Performance Indicators (KPIs) 187
    10.3 Web Analytics Tools (Google Analytics) 191
    10.4 Data Analysis And Interpretation 195
    10.5 Reporting And Performance Optimization 199

Foreword

I have the equivalent of an Oscar in digital marketing. I was Top Influencer, Social Media Week 2012, the top event in the space, today reaching 700 million people globally, simultaneously held in 26 top global cities for a week.

All marketing eventually is going to be digital. Already a big chunk of it is.

This is not a book to be read from cover to cover, although that is also an option. This is more a handbook that you dive into for portions most relevant to you at any given time.

I consult. And this handbook allows me to have meaningful conversations with my clients.

Many suggestions spread all across the book are but starting points. And hence the title: Digital Marketing Minimum.

May 2024.

1. Introduction To Digital Marketing

Digital marketing is the strategic use of online platforms and techniques to promote products or services, engage with audiences, and drive business growth in the digital realm.

1.1 What is Digital Marketing?

Digital marketing refers to the strategic use of various online channels and technologies to promote products, services, or brands and engage with a targeted audience. It encompasses a wide range of tactics, techniques, and methodologies that leverage digital platforms and tools to achieve marketing objectives.

In today's increasingly digital world, where people are spending more time online and using digital devices to access information, make purchases, and interact with others, businesses and marketers have recognized the immense potential of digital marketing. Unlike traditional marketing methods that rely on offline channels like print media, television, or radio, digital marketing harnesses the power of the internet and digital technologies to reach and connect with a vast audience in a more targeted and measurable manner.

At its core, digital marketing is centered around the concept of creating a strong online presence and establishing meaningful connections with potential customers. By leveraging digital channels such as websites, search engines, social media, email, mobile apps, and various other online platforms, businesses can effectively communicate their brand message, generate leads, drive website traffic, and ultimately increase conversions and sales.

Digital marketing encompasses a wide range of strategies and tactics, some of which include:

1. Search Engine Optimization (SEO): SEO involves optimizing a website's content, structure, and technical aspects to improve its visibility and ranking in search engine results. By targeting relevant keywords and optimizing for user experience, businesses can attract organic (non-paid) traffic from search engines.

2. Pay-Per-Click Advertising (PPC): PPC advertising involves placing paid advertisements on search engines and other digital platforms. Advertisers only pay when their ads are clicked, making it a cost-effective way to drive targeted traffic to a website and increase brand visibility.

3. Social Media Marketing: Social media platforms such as Facebook, Instagram, Twitter, and LinkedIn offer powerful avenues for businesses to engage with their audience, build brand awareness, and foster customer loyalty. Social media marketing involves creating and sharing valuable content, running targeted ad campaigns, and leveraging user-generated content to promote products or services.

4. Content Marketing: Content marketing focuses on creating and distributing valuable, relevant, and consistent content to attract and retain a clearly defined audience. This can take the form of blog posts, articles, videos, infographics, podcasts, and more. The goal is to provide valuable information, establish thought leadership, and ultimately drive customer engagement and conversions.

5. Email Marketing: Email marketing involves sending targeted messages and promotional content directly to a subscriber's inbox. With personalized and segmented campaigns, businesses can nurture leads, build customer relationships, and drive conversions. Email marketing is highly effective for building brand loyalty and driving repeat purchases.

6. Influencer Marketing: Influencer marketing leverages the influence and reach of popular individuals or organizations within a specific niche to promote products or services. By partnering with influencers, brands can tap into their credibility and audience trust to increase brand awareness and drive conversions.

7. Mobile Marketing: With the widespread use of smartphones and mobile devices, mobile marketing focuses on reaching and engaging users on their mobile platforms. This includes strategies such as mobile advertising, mobile-responsive website design, mobile apps, and location-based marketing.

8. Analytics and Data-driven Insights: Digital marketing provides robust tools and analytics platforms to measure, track, and analyze various aspects of campaigns. By analyzing data and metrics, marketers can gain valuable insights into consumer behavior, campaign performance, and make data-driven decisions to optimize marketing efforts.

Digital marketing offers several advantages over traditional marketing methods. It provides a higher level of measurability, allowing marketers to track and analyze the effectiveness of campaigns in real-time. It also offers greater targeting capabilities, enabling businesses to reach specific demographics, interests, and behaviors. Digital marketing campaigns are often more cost-effective than traditional advertising, as they can be tailored to suit different budgets and objectives.

In conclusion, digital marketing has revolutionized the way businesses promote and market their products or services. It offers a wide range of strategies and channels to connect with a targeted audience, build brand awareness, and drive conversions. As the digital landscape continues to evolve, staying up-to-date with the latest trends and best practices in digital marketing is crucial for businesses to remain competitive in the online marketplace.

1.2 Evolution of Digital Marketing

The Evolution of Digital Marketing: From the Early Days to the Modern Landscape

Introduction:

Digital marketing has come a long way since its inception, transforming the way businesses engage with their audience and promote their products or services. The evolution of digital marketing has been driven by advancements in technology, changing consumer behaviors, and the growing importance of online platforms. In this article, we will explore the key milestones in the evolution of digital marketing, from its early days to the modern landscape.

1. The Emergence of the Internet:

The journey of digital marketing begins with the emergence of the internet. In the 1990s, the internet became widely accessible, leading to a new era of communication and information sharing. This created opportunities for businesses to connect with a global audience and sparked the need for online marketing strategies.

2. Rise of Search Engines and SEO:

The early 2000s witnessed the rise of search engines, with Google leading the pack. Search engine optimization (SEO) emerged as a crucial aspect of digital marketing, as businesses recognized the importance of appearing prominently in search results. SEO focused on optimizing websites to improve their visibility and rankings, laying the foundation for organic online marketing.

3. Pay-Per-Click Advertising (PPC) and SEM:

As the internet became more commercialized, pay-per-click (PPC) advertising gained prominence. Search engine marketing (SEM) allowed businesses to place targeted ads on search engine results pages, paying only when users clicked on their ads. This form of advertising offered immediate visibility and measurable results, providing marketers with more control over their campaigns.

4. Social Media Revolution:

The advent of social media platforms such as Facebook, Twitter, and LinkedIn transformed the digital marketing landscape. Businesses realized the potential of engaging with their audience directly on these platforms, leading to the rise of social media marketing. Brands began building online communities, sharing content, and leveraging social ads to reach their target demographics. The ability to connect and engage with customers on a personal level opened new doors for relationship-building and brand loyalty.

5. Mobile Marketing and the Rise of Apps:

The proliferation of smartphones led to a significant shift in consumer behavior. Mobile marketing gained momentum as businesses recognized the need to optimize their online presence for mobile devices. Mobile-responsive websites, mobile ads, and mobile apps became crucial components of digital marketing strategies. Mobile apps, in particular, allowed brands to provide personalized experiences, gather user data, and deliver targeted messaging.

6. Personalization and Data-driven Marketing:

With the advancement of technology, data-driven marketing became a game-changer. Marketers could access and analyze vast amounts of data to understand consumer preferences, behaviors, and purchase patterns. This allowed for highly personalized and targeted marketing campaigns, enhancing customer experiences and increasing conversion rates.

Personalization became a cornerstone of digital marketing, with tailored content, recommendations, and email campaigns becoming the norm.

7. Video Marketing and Influencer Marketing:

Video marketing has witnessed explosive growth in recent years, thanks to the popularity of platforms like YouTube and the integration of video content on social media. Videos have become a powerful tool for storytelling, engaging audiences, and conveying brand messages. Influencer marketing also gained traction, with businesses partnering with popular individuals or social media personalities to leverage their influence and reach.

8. Artificial Intelligence (AI) and Automation:

Artificial intelligence (AI) and automation have revolutionized digital marketing, enabling marketers to streamline processes, personalize experiences, and optimize campaigns. AI-powered chatbots, automated email marketing, and predictive analytics have become valuable assets for marketers, allowing for efficient and data-driven decision-making.

Conclusion:

The evolution of digital marketing has been a remarkable journey, shaped by technological advancements and changing consumer behaviors. From the early days of the internet to the modern landscape dominated by social media, mobile devices, personalization, and AI, digital marketing continues to evolve at a rapid pace. As businesses adapt to this ever-changing landscape, staying informed about emerging trends and embracing new technologies will be vital for success in the digital realm. The future of digital marketing holds exciting possibilities, with emerging technologies such as virtual reality (VR), augmented reality (AR), and voice search poised to further reshape the digital marketing landscape.

1.3 Benefits of Digital Marketing

Unleashing the Power: Exploring the Benefits of Digital Marketing

Introduction:

In today's digitally connected world, digital marketing has become a cornerstone for businesses of all sizes and industries. Leveraging online platforms and technologies, digital marketing offers a myriad of benefits that can transform the way businesses engage with their audience, promote their products or services, and drive growth. In this article, we will delve into the extensive range of benefits that digital marketing brings to the table.

1. Enhanced Targeting and Reach:

One of the primary advantages of digital marketing is the ability to precisely target and reach specific audiences. Through data-driven strategies, businesses can segment their target market based on demographics, interests, behavior, and other relevant factors. This level of targeting ensures that marketing efforts are directed towards individuals who are most likely to be interested in the products or services being offered, resulting in higher conversion rates and ROI.

2. Cost-Effectiveness:

Compared to traditional marketing methods, digital marketing offers a more cost-effective solution for businesses. With digital channels such as social media, search engines, and email marketing, businesses can reach a wide audience at a fraction of the cost required for traditional advertising. Additionally, digital marketing allows for precise budget control, as businesses can set spending limits, choose cost-per-click (CPC) or cost-per-thousand-impressions (CPM) models, and monitor campaign performance in real-time.

3. Measurable Results and Analytics:

One of the significant advantages of digital marketing is the ability to measure and analyze the results of marketing campaigns accurately. Digital analytics tools provide detailed insights into key performance indicators (KPIs) such as website traffic, conversions, click-through rates (CTR), engagement metrics, and more. This data-driven approach empowers businesses to optimize their marketing strategies, identify areas of improvement, and make data-backed decisions for future campaigns.

4. Improved Customer Engagement and Interaction:

Digital marketing facilitates direct and meaningful engagement with customers. Through social media platforms, email marketing, live chat, and interactive content, businesses can establish two-way communication channels with their audience. This creates opportunities for personalized interactions, addressing customer queries, building brand loyalty, and gathering valuable feedback. The ability to engage customers in real-time fosters stronger relationships and enhances the overall customer experience.

5. Global Reach and 24/7 Availability:

Unlike traditional marketing, digital marketing allows businesses to transcend geographical boundaries and reach a global audience. With a well-optimized website, businesses can attract visitors from anywhere in the world, expanding their customer base and potential market share. Furthermore, digital marketing operates 24/7, enabling businesses to connect with customers at any time, irrespective of time zones. This constant availability ensures that businesses can capture leads, nurture relationships, and drive conversions around the clock.

6. Flexibility and Adaptability:

Digital marketing provides flexibility and adaptability, allowing businesses to respond quickly to market trends, consumer behavior, and competitor strategies. Campaigns can be modified and adjusted in real-time, enabling businesses to optimize their messaging, targeting, and budget allocation for maximum impact. Additionally, digital marketing allows for A/B testing, where different variations of content, designs, or offers can be tested simultaneously to identify the most effective approach.

7. Brand Building and Reputation Management:

Digital marketing plays a pivotal role in building brand awareness and managing brand reputation. Through consistent messaging, storytelling, and content creation, businesses can shape their brand identity and establish a strong online presence. Social media platforms, online reviews, and customer testimonials provide opportunities for businesses to engage in brand advocacy, address concerns, and manage their online reputation effectively.

8. Integration and Synergy:

Digital marketing channels can be seamlessly integrated to create a holistic and synergistic approach. A well-executed digital marketing strategy leverages multiple channels, such as search engine optimization (SEO), content marketing, social media, email marketing, and PPC advertising, to reinforce brand messaging and maximize reach. Integration also enables businesses to leverage the strengths of each channel, creating a cohesive marketing ecosystem that amplifies results.

Conclusion:

The benefits of digital marketing are vast and game-changing for businesses seeking to thrive in the digital age. From precise targeting and cost-effectiveness to measurable results, improved customer engagement, and global reach, digital marketing empowers businesses to connect with their audience on a deeper level and drive sustainable growth. By leveraging the advantages of digital marketing, businesses can stay ahead of the competition, adapt to evolving consumer behaviors, and capitalize on the limitless opportunities offered by the digital landscape. As digital marketing continues to evolve, businesses must embrace its potential and leverage the power of digital channels to unlock unprecedented success.

1.4 Key Digital Marketing Terminologies

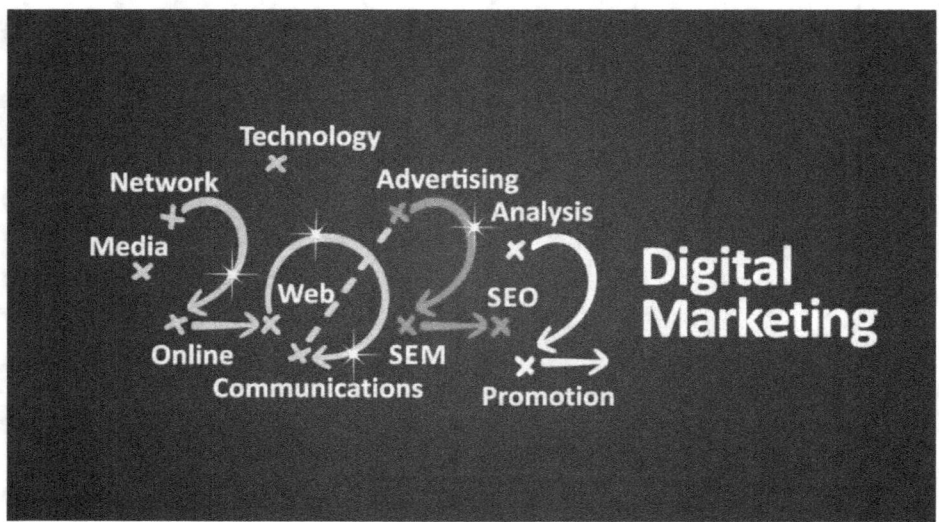

Decoding the Digital Jargon: Essential Digital Marketing Terminologies

Introduction:

Digital marketing is a dynamic and ever-evolving field that is accompanied by a vast array of terminologies. Familiarizing yourself with these key digital marketing terms is essential for understanding and effectively implementing digital marketing strategies. In this article, we will delve into the essential terminologies that every digital marketer should be familiar with.

1. Search Engine Optimization (SEO):

Search Engine Optimization, commonly known as SEO, refers to the practice of optimizing websites and webpages to improve their visibility and ranking on search engine results pages (SERPs). This involves various techniques, including keyword research, on-page optimization, off-page optimization, and technical optimizations, with the goal of driving organic (non-paid) traffic to a website.

2. Pay-Per-Click (PPC) Advertising:

Pay-Per-Click advertising, or PPC, is an online advertising model where advertisers pay a fee each time their ad is clicked. It is commonly associated with search engine advertising, where businesses bid on keywords to display their ads in search engine results. PPC campaigns offer immediate visibility and allow businesses to target specific keywords, demographics, and locations.

3. Conversion Rate Optimization (CRO):

Conversion Rate Optimization, or CRO, is the practice of increasing the percentage of website visitors who take a desired action, such as making a purchase, filling out a form, or subscribing to a newsletter. CRO involves analyzing user behavior, conducting A/B testing, and making data-driven changes to improve the conversion rate and overall effectiveness of a website.

4. Key Performance Indicators (KPIs):

Key Performance Indicators, or KPIs, are measurable values used to evaluate the success of marketing campaigns and strategies. KPIs vary depending on the specific goals of a business and can include metrics such as website traffic, conversion rate, bounce rate, click-through rate, return on investment (ROI), and customer lifetime value (CLV). Setting and tracking relevant KPIs help businesses assess performance and make informed decisions.

5. Return on Investment (ROI):

Return on Investment, or ROI, is a metric used to measure the profitability and effectiveness of a marketing investment. It calculates the ratio of the net profit generated from a campaign or initiative to the cost of that campaign. A positive ROI indicates that the marketing investment has yielded a profit, while a negative ROI implies a loss. ROI analysis helps businesses allocate resources effectively and determine the success of their marketing efforts.

6. Call-to-Action (CTA):

A Call-to-Action, or CTA, is a prompt or instruction designed to encourage an immediate response from the viewer or reader. CTAs are typically used in digital marketing to guide users towards a desired action, such as "Buy Now," "Subscribe," or "Download Now." Effective CTAs are clear, compelling, and strategically placed to drive conversions and engage users.

7. Engagement Rate:

Engagement Rate is a metric used to measure the level of interaction and involvement that users have with digital content or campaigns. It is typically calculated by dividing the total number of engagements (likes, comments, shares, etc.) by the total number of impressions or followers and expressing the result as a percentage. Engagement rate is a key indicator of content quality, audience interest, and the overall success of social media and content marketing efforts.

8. Return on Ad Spend (ROAS):

Return on Ad Spend, or ROAS, is a metric used to measure the effectiveness of advertising campaigns, particularly in PPC advertising. It calculates the revenue generated from an advertising campaign divided by the cost of that campaign. ROAS provides insights into the profitability of specific advertising channels, keywords, or campaigns, helping businesses optimize their advertising strategies and allocate budgets accordingly.

Conclusion:

Familiarizing yourself with key digital marketing terminologies is crucial for navigating the dynamic landscape of digital marketing effectively. Understanding these terms enables marketers to communicate, strategize, and analyze digital marketing efforts with clarity and precision. From SEO and PPC to CRO, KPIs, and engagement rate, these terminologies form the foundation of digital marketing knowledge. As the digital marketing landscape continues to evolve, staying up-to-date with new terminologies and industry trends will be vital for success in the ever-changing digital realm.

1.5 Overview of Digital Marketing Channels

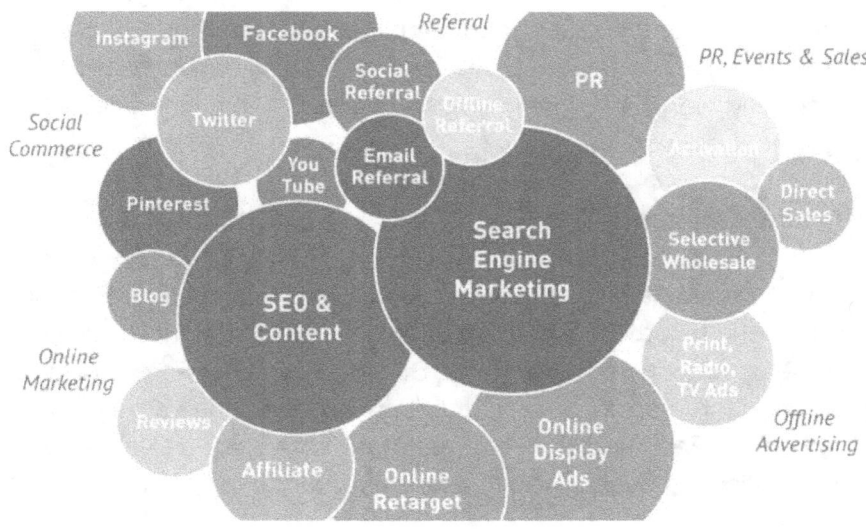

A Comprehensive Overview of Digital Marketing Channels

Introduction:

Digital marketing offers a multitude of channels that enable businesses to reach their target audience, engage with potential customers, and promote their products or services effectively. Each digital marketing channel presents unique opportunities and strategies to connect with consumers in the digital realm. In this article, we will provide a comprehensive overview of the key digital marketing channels that businesses can leverage to enhance their online presence and drive business growth.

1. Search Engine Marketing (SEM):

Search Engine Marketing, or SEM, encompasses strategies that focus on increasing a website's visibility in search engine results pages (SERPs) through paid advertising. SEM involves pay-per-click (PPC) campaigns, where businesses bid on relevant keywords to display their ads prominently. Popular platforms for SEM include Google Ads and Bing Ads. SEM allows businesses to target specific keywords and demographics, driving targeted traffic and increasing brand visibility.

2. Search Engine Optimization (SEO):

Search Engine Optimization, or SEO, is the practice of optimizing a website to improve its organic (non-paid) visibility in search engine results. SEO involves various techniques, including keyword research, on-page optimization, off-page optimization, and technical optimizations. By aligning their website with search engine algorithms, businesses can increase their chances of ranking higher in organic search results, driving consistent and relevant traffic to their website.

3. Social Media Marketing:

Social Media Marketing leverages social media platforms such as Facebook, Instagram, Twitter, LinkedIn, and others to engage with audiences, build brand awareness, and drive conversions. Businesses can create and share compelling content, run targeted ad campaigns, and engage with followers to foster relationships. Each social media platform offers unique features and demographics, allowing businesses to tailor their marketing efforts to their target audience.

4. Content Marketing:

Content Marketing involves creating and distributing valuable, relevant, and informative content to attract and engage a target audience. This can take the form of blog posts, articles, videos, infographics, podcasts, and more. Content marketing builds brand authority, fosters customer loyalty, and drives organic traffic. It focuses on providing value to the audience, addressing their pain points, and establishing thought leadership within the industry.

5. Email Marketing:

Email Marketing utilizes email to deliver targeted messages and promotional content to subscribers. With personalized and segmented campaigns, businesses can nurture leads, build customer relationships, and drive conversions. Email marketing allows for automation, personalization, and the ability to track engagement metrics. It is an effective channel for delivering personalized offers, news updates, and nurturing customer loyalty.

6. Pay-Per-Click Advertising (PPC):

Pay-Per-Click Advertising, or PPC, involves placing paid advertisements on search engines, social media platforms, and other digital channels. Advertisers only pay when their ads are clicked, making it a cost-effective way to drive targeted traffic to a website. Platforms like Google Ads, Bing

Ads, Facebook Ads, and Twitter Ads provide sophisticated targeting options, allowing businesses to reach their desired audience with precision.

7. Display Advertising:

Display Advertising encompasses graphical advertisements that are displayed on websites, apps, or social media platforms. These ads can be in the form of banners, images, videos, or interactive media. Display advertising allows businesses to increase brand awareness, drive traffic, and target specific demographics or interests. Ad networks, such as Google Display Network and programmatic advertising platforms, provide extensive reach and targeting capabilities.

8. Influencer Marketing:

Influencer Marketing leverages the popularity and reach of influential individuals or organizations within a specific niche to promote products or services. Businesses collaborate with influencers to tap into their credibility and engage with their audience. Influencer marketing can take various forms, including sponsored content, brand collaborations, product reviews, and endorsements. It allows businesses to reach a targeted audience and leverage the trust and authenticity associated with influencers.

Conclusion:

Digital marketing channels offer diverse opportunities for businesses to connect with their target audience, drive engagement, and achieve marketing objectives. Each channel has its strengths and strategies, allowing businesses to tailor their approach based on their goals and target demographics. By leveraging a combination of search engine marketing, social media marketing, content marketing, email marketing, pay-per-click advertising, display advertising, and influencer marketing, businesses can create a robust and holistic digital marketing strategy that maximizes their reach and impact. As the digital landscape evolves, businesses must stay informed about emerging channels and adapt their strategies to remain competitive and effectively engage with their target audience.

2. Website Optimization and Design

Website optimization and design improve performance, usability, and aesthetics to attract visitors, enhance user experience, and achieve business goals.

2.1 Importance of Website Optimization

Unlocking Success: The Importance of Website Optimization

Introduction:

In the digital age, a website serves as a crucial touchpoint between businesses and their audience. A well-optimized website not only enhances user experience but also plays a pivotal role in driving traffic, conversions, and overall business success. Website optimization involves various strategies and techniques aimed at improving website performance, visibility, and user satisfaction. In this article, we will explore the key reasons why website optimization is essential for businesses in today's competitive online landscape.

1. Enhanced User Experience:

Website optimization focuses on delivering a seamless and user-friendly experience to visitors. An optimized website ensures fast loading times, intuitive navigation, responsive design, and mobile compatibility. A positive user experience fosters engagement, encourages visitors to explore the website further, and increases the likelihood of conversions.

2. Improved Search Engine Visibility:

Search engine optimization (SEO) is a critical component of website optimization. Optimizing a website's structure, content, and technical aspects in line with SEO best practices helps search engines understand and index the website more effectively. This, in turn, improves the website's visibility in search engine results, leading to increased organic traffic and higher chances of attracting relevant visitors.

3. Higher Conversion Rates:

A well-optimized website is designed to guide visitors through a seamless journey, leading them towards the desired actions, such as making a purchase, submitting a form, or subscribing to a newsletter. Elements like clear calls-to-action, well-placed contact forms, and persuasive copywriting contribute to higher conversion rates. Website optimization focuses on removing barriers, streamlining the conversion process, and instilling trust and confidence in visitors.

4. Mobile-Friendly Experience:

With the widespread use of mobile devices, optimizing a website for mobile viewing has become imperative. A mobile-friendly website adapts to different screen sizes and resolutions, ensuring a consistent and enjoyable experience for users on smartphones and tablets. Given that mobile usage continues to rise, a mobile-friendly website is crucial for reaching and engaging with the ever-growing mobile audience.

5. Decreased Bounce Rates:

Website optimization plays a significant role in reducing bounce rates. By improving page load times, enhancing content relevance, and optimizing navigation, visitors are more likely to stay on the website for longer periods. A lower bounce rate indicates that visitors find value in the website, explore multiple pages, and engage with the content, ultimately increasing the chances of conversion and achieving business goals.

6. Competitive Advantage:

In a crowded online marketplace, businesses must differentiate themselves from competitors. A well-optimized website gives businesses a competitive advantage by providing a superior user experience, improved search engine visibility, and better overall performance. By optimizing website elements like site speed, usability, and design, businesses can stand out, attract more visitors, and gain an edge over competitors.

7. Data-Driven Decision Making:

Website optimization involves leveraging analytics tools and tracking user behavior to gain valuable insights. By analyzing data related to website traffic, user interactions, and conversions, businesses can make informed decisions about optimizing specific website elements, improving marketing strategies, and enhancing the overall user experience. Data-driven decision making helps businesses identify strengths, weaknesses, and opportunities for improvement, leading to continuous growth and success.

8. Brand Reputation and Trust:

A well-optimized website enhances a brand's reputation and instills trust in visitors. A professional, aesthetically pleasing design, easy navigation, and relevant, high-quality content create a positive impression of the brand. A website that functions smoothly and provides a secure browsing experience reinforces trust and confidence in users, making them more likely to engage with the brand and become loyal customers.

Conclusion:

Website optimization is an integral aspect of digital marketing that cannot be overlooked in today's online landscape. From providing an exceptional user experience and improving search engine visibility to increasing conversion rates and gaining a competitive advantage, website optimization is vital for businesses seeking to succeed in the digital realm. By investing in website optimization strategies and continually refining the website based on user feedback and data-driven insights, businesses can unlock the full potential of their online presence, attract more visitors, and drive sustainable growth in an increasingly digital world.

2.2 User Experience (UX) Design Principles

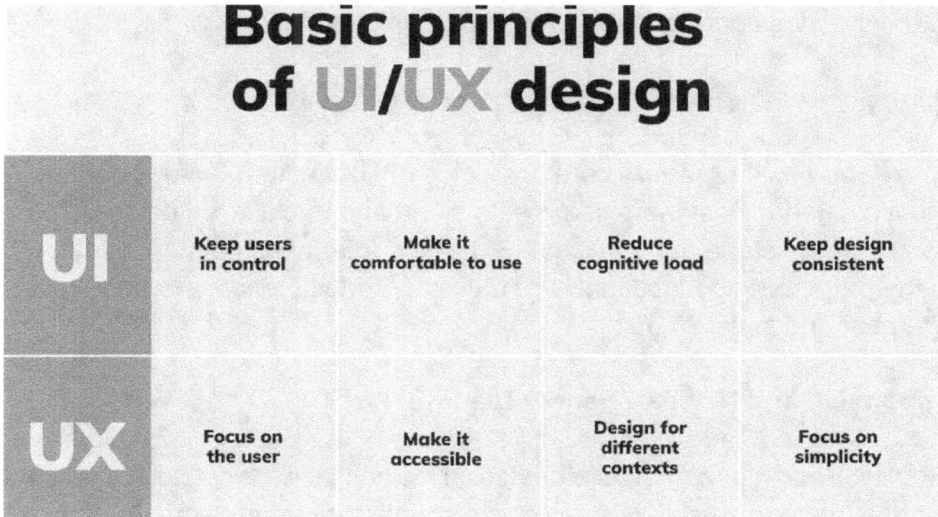

Crafting Memorable Experiences: User Experience (UX) Design Principles

Introduction:

User Experience (UX) design is a critical aspect of creating digital products and websites that deliver exceptional experiences to users. UX design principles focus on understanding user needs, behaviors, and preferences to create intuitive, enjoyable, and effective designs. In this article, we will explore the key UX design principles that guide designers in crafting memorable experiences for users.

1. User-Centered Design:

User-centered design is the foundation of UX design principles. It involves placing the needs, goals, and expectations of users at the forefront of the design process. By understanding the target audience through research, personas, and user testing, designers can create designs that align with user preferences and deliver meaningful experiences.

2. Clear and Consistent Navigation:

Navigation plays a vital role in guiding users through a digital product or website. Clear and consistent navigation ensures that users can easily find and access the information they need. This involves logical menu structures, intuitive icons, and descriptive labels that communicate the purpose of each element. Consistency in navigation across different sections of the product or website enhances usability and reduces cognitive load.

3. Simplicity and Minimalism:

Simplicity and minimalism are core principles of UX design. By focusing on essential elements, designers can create clean and uncluttered designs that are easy to understand and navigate. Simplified interfaces help users quickly grasp the purpose and functionality of a digital product, leading to better user engagement and satisfaction.

4. Responsive and Mobile-Friendly Design:

With the increasing use of mobile devices, responsive and mobile-friendly design has become crucial. UX designers optimize designs to ensure they adapt seamlessly to different screen sizes and resolutions. This enables users to have consistent and enjoyable experiences across various devices, promoting accessibility and user engagement.

5. Consistency in Visual Design:

Consistency in visual design is essential for establishing a cohesive and recognizable brand identity. Designers employ consistent color palettes, typography, iconography, and layout throughout a digital product or website. Consistency enhances user familiarity, reduces confusion, and builds trust in the brand.

6. Accessibility and Inclusivity:

Accessibility is a critical aspect of UX design, ensuring that digital products and websites are usable by individuals with disabilities. Designers follow accessibility guidelines, including providing alternative text for images, incorporating proper color contrast, and offering keyboard navigation options. By making designs accessible and inclusive, designers enable a broader audience to engage with and benefit from digital experiences.

7. Feedback and Responsiveness:

Providing timely feedback and responsiveness to user actions is essential for a positive user experience. Designers implement interactive elements, visual cues, and notifications to communicate system responses and guide users through their interactions. Instant feedback assures users that their actions are recognized, reducing uncertainty and enhancing engagement.

8. User Testing and Iterative Design:

User testing is a vital part of the UX design process. Designers conduct usability tests, gather feedback, and iterate designs based on user insights. This iterative approach allows designers to continuously refine and improve the user experience, ensuring that designs align with user needs and expectations.

9. Emotional Design:

Emotional design considers the user's emotional response to a digital product or website. By incorporating elements such as color psychology, visual aesthetics, and storytelling, designers evoke positive emotions and establish an emotional connection with users. This enhances user engagement, satisfaction, and brand loyalty.

10. Performance and Speed Optimization:

Performance and speed are critical aspects of UX design. Slow-loading pages and laggy interactions frustrate users and diminish the overall experience. UX designers optimize designs to minimize loading times, optimize assets, and ensure smooth interactions, providing users with a seamless and efficient experience.

Conclusion:

User Experience (UX) design principles guide designers in creating digital products and websites that prioritize user needs, behaviors, and preferences. By embracing principles such as user-centered design, clear navigation, simplicity, responsiveness, and accessibility, designers can craft memorable experiences that engage users and deliver value. The ongoing process of user testing, iterative design, and attention to emotional design further refines the user experience. By adhering to these principles, businesses can differentiate themselves, build trust with users, and foster long-term relationships in an increasingly competitive digital landscape.

2.3 Responsive Web Design

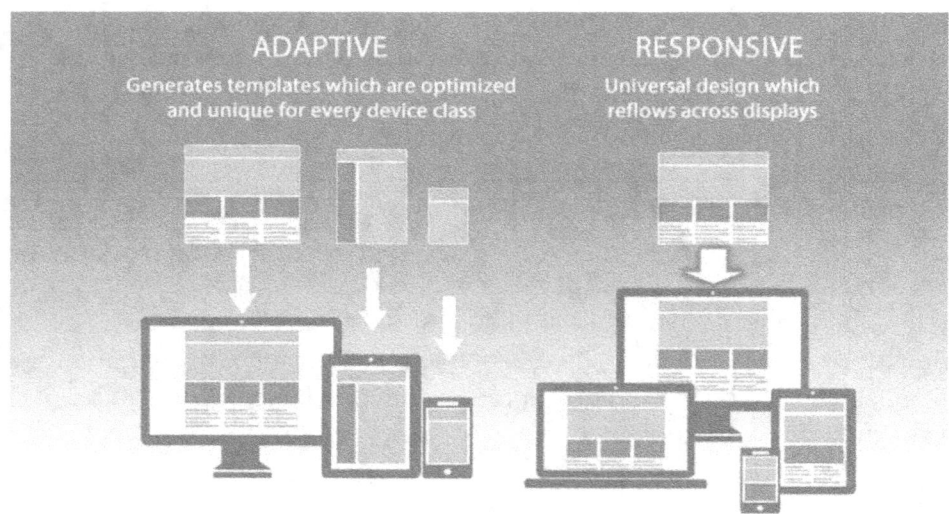

Embracing the Future: Responsive Web Design for Optimal User Experiences

Introduction:

In the age of diverse devices and screen sizes, responsive web design has become a fundamental approach to creating websites that adapt seamlessly to various devices and provide optimal user experiences. Responsive web design focuses on building flexible and adaptable websites that automatically adjust layout, content, and functionality to ensure a consistent and user-friendly experience across desktops, tablets, and mobile devices. In this article, we will explore the principles, benefits, and best practices of responsive web design.

1. Understanding Responsive Web Design:

Responsive web design is an approach that enables websites to respond and adapt to different screen sizes, resolutions, and orientations. It employs a combination of fluid grids, flexible images, and media queries to automatically adjust the layout and content based on the user's device. By embracing responsive design, websites can provide a seamless experience, regardless of the device being used.

2. Fluid Grids and Flexible Layouts:

A key aspect of responsive web design is the use of fluid grids and flexible layouts. Rather than relying on fixed pixel-based measurements, responsive designs utilize relative units such as percentages and ems to allow elements to scale proportionally. This ensures that content adapts and rearranges itself to fit different screen sizes, maintaining a visually pleasing and functional layout.

3. Media Queries and Breakpoints:

Media queries play a vital role in responsive web design. They enable websites to apply specific CSS rules based on the characteristics of the user's device, such as screen width, height, and resolution. By defining breakpoints, designers can specify different layout and styling rules to accommodate various screen sizes. This ensures that the website adapts smoothly and delivers an optimized experience across different devices.

4. Mobile-First Approach:

Adopting a mobile-first approach is a common strategy in responsive web design. This approach prioritizes the design and optimization of the mobile experience first and then progressively enhances the design for larger screens. By starting with a mobile-focused design, businesses ensure that their websites are lightweight, fast-loading, and optimized for smaller screens. It also allows for a more streamlined and efficient design process.

5. Content Prioritization and Hierarchy:

Responsive web design encourages designers to prioritize and structure content based on its importance and relevance. With limited screen space on mobile devices, designers must carefully consider what content should be prioritized and how it should be displayed. This involves optimizing navigation menus, condensing text, and employing collapsible elements to ensure a seamless and intuitive user experience across devices.

6. Images and Media Optimization:

Responsive web design requires careful consideration of images and media. Large and high-resolution images can significantly impact page loading times and consume excessive data on mobile devices. Designers utilize techniques such as responsive images, lazy loading, and compressing image file sizes to ensure optimal performance across devices without compromising visual quality.

7. Testing and Iteration:

Thorough testing across various devices and screen sizes is crucial to ensure the effectiveness of responsive web design. Designers should regularly test and iterate the design to identify any potential issues or inconsistencies. Usability testing, performance testing, and cross-device compatibility checks enable designers to make data-driven decisions and refine the responsive design for optimal user experiences.

8. Benefits of Responsive Web Design:

Responsive web design offers numerous benefits for businesses and users alike. It ensures a consistent brand experience, reduces development and maintenance costs by eliminating the need for separate mobile websites or apps, and improves search engine optimization (SEO) by providing a single URL for all devices. For users, responsive design delivers a seamless and user-friendly experience, eliminating the need for zooming, scrolling, or horizontal navigation.

Conclusion:

Responsive web design has become an essential approach in creating websites that cater to the diverse range of devices and screen sizes in today's digital landscape. By employing fluid grids, flexible layouts, media queries, and a mobile-first approach, businesses can provide optimal user experiences across devices, improving engagement, conversion rates, and brand loyalty. With careful attention to content prioritization, media optimization, and rigorous testing, responsive web design enables businesses to adapt to evolving user preferences and technological advancements. Embracing responsive design is not only a strategic choice but a necessity to meet the expectations of users and stay ahead in the ever-evolving digital realm.

2.4 Website Navigation and Structure

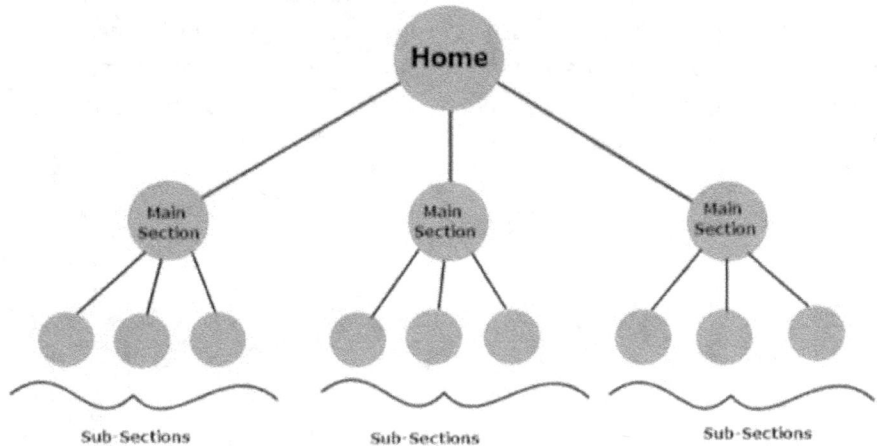

Navigating Success: Optimizing Website Navigation and Structure

Introduction:

Website navigation and structure are fundamental elements of a successful website that contribute to user experience, engagement, and conversion rates. A well-designed navigation system and intuitive structure ensure that visitors can easily find the information they need, navigate through the website effortlessly, and achieve their goals. In this article, we will explore the key principles, best practices, and strategies for optimizing website navigation and structure.

1. Clear and Consistent Navigation:

Clear and consistent navigation is crucial for providing a seamless browsing experience. The navigation menu should be prominently displayed, easy to find, and use intuitive labels that accurately represent the content and sections of the website. Consistency in navigation across all pages ensures familiarity and reduces user confusion.

2. Logical Information Architecture:

A well-structured information architecture is essential for organizing content in a logical and hierarchical manner. Categorize and group related content together, ensuring that users can navigate through sections and sub-sections easily. This helps users understand the website's structure and find relevant information efficiently.

3. User-Centric Design:

Website navigation and structure should prioritize the needs and expectations of users. Conduct user research to understand their goals, behaviors, and preferred browsing patterns. Design the navigation system based on these insights, ensuring that users can find information quickly and easily.

4. Simplicity and Efficiency:

Simplicity is key to effective website navigation. Avoid overwhelming users with too many menu options or complex navigation systems. Keep the navigation concise, focused, and streamlined. Ensure that users can reach any page within a few clicks, minimizing the number of steps required to find desired information.

5. Responsive and Mobile-Friendly Design:

With the increasing use of mobile devices, responsive and mobile-friendly design is essential. Optimize navigation for smaller screens by employing responsive design techniques, such as collapsible menus or hamburger icons. Ensure that navigation elements are easily tappable and that the overall layout adapts seamlessly to different screen sizes.

6. Visual Hierarchy and Prioritization:

Visual hierarchy plays a significant role in guiding users' attention and helping them navigate through a website. Use size, color, typography, and spacing to create a clear visual hierarchy that highlights important navigation elements and content. Prioritize crucial information and sections to ensure they are easily discoverable.

7. Breadcrumb Navigation:

Breadcrumb navigation provides users with a trail of their current location within the website. It helps users understand the website's structure and provides an easy way to navigate back to previous pages. Breadcrumbs are especially useful for websites with complex hierarchies or extensive content.

8. User-Friendly Search Functionality:

Implementing a user-friendly search functionality enhances website navigation. Incorporate a search bar prominently on the website, ensuring that it is easily accessible and intuitive to use. Provide relevant search suggestions, autocomplete, and filters to help users find specific content or products efficiently.

9. Contextual Links and Calls-to-Action:

Contextual links and calls-to-action within the content guide users to related pages or actions, further enhancing website navigation. Linking relevant keywords or phrases to related content encourages exploration and keeps users engaged within the website. Well-designed calls-to-action prompt users to take specific actions, leading them to relevant sections or conversion points.

10. Continuous Testing and Iteration:

Continuous testing and iteration are essential for refining website navigation and structure. Conduct usability testing to gather user feedback, analyze website analytics, and track user behavior to identify areas for improvement. A data-driven approach allows for ongoing optimization, ensuring the navigation system evolves with user needs and preferences.

Conclusion:

Optimizing website navigation and structure is integral to creating a user-friendly and successful website. By implementing clear and consistent navigation, employing logical information architecture, and focusing on user-centric design, businesses can provide an intuitive browsing experience that leads to increased engagement and conversions. Prioritizing simplicity, responsiveness, visual hierarchy, and user-friendly search functionality further enhances website navigation. Continuous testing, analysis, and iteration enable businesses to adapt to evolving user preferences and ensure that the website navigation and structure align with user needs. By investing time and effort into optimizing website navigation and structure, businesses can create a memorable user experience, foster trust, and achieve their goals in the competitive digital landscape.

2.5 Conversion Rate Optimization (CRO)

Unlocking Success: The Power of Conversion Rate Optimization (CRO)

Introduction:

In the realm of digital marketing, conversion rate optimization (CRO) has emerged as a vital strategy for businesses looking to maximize the value of their website traffic. CRO involves the systematic process of enhancing website elements, user experience, and marketing strategies to increase the percentage of visitors who take desired actions, such as making a purchase, filling out a form, or subscribing to a newsletter. In this article, we will explore the significance of conversion rate optimization, its key principles, and best practices to help businesses unlock the full potential of their website and drive meaningful results.

1. Understanding Conversion Rate Optimization:

Conversion rate optimization is a data-driven approach aimed at improving the performance of a website or marketing campaign by increasing the conversion rate. The conversion rate is calculated by dividing the number of conversions by the total number of website visitors, expressed as a percentage. CRO focuses on identifying and eliminating barriers or friction points in the user journey, optimizing key elements, and implementing strategies to enhance the likelihood of conversions.

2. Setting Clear Goals and Metrics:

The foundation of successful CRO lies in setting clear goals and metrics. Businesses must define what actions they consider as conversions and establish key performance indicators (KPIs) to measure and track the effectiveness of their CRO efforts. These goals can range from increasing sales or leads to improving engagement or reducing bounce rates. By aligning goals with metrics, businesses can monitor progress and make data-driven decisions to optimize conversion rates.

3. Conducting Data Analysis:

Data analysis forms the backbone of CRO. Businesses must collect and analyze relevant data to gain insights into user behavior, identify areas of improvement, and prioritize optimization efforts. Tools like Google Analytics, heatmaps, user recordings, and A/B testing platforms provide valuable data and insights to understand user interactions, conversion funnel drop-offs, and areas of friction.

4. Optimizing User Experience:

User experience plays a critical role in conversion rate optimization. By improving website navigation, reducing page load times, simplifying forms, and enhancing overall usability, businesses can create a seamless and intuitive experience for visitors. A positive user experience fosters trust, reduces bounce rates, and encourages visitors to take desired actions.

5. A/B Testing and Experimentation:

A/B testing is a fundamental technique in CRO that involves comparing two versions (A and B) of a webpage or element to determine which performs better in terms of conversions. By testing and iterating various design elements, content variations, calls-to-action, and layout options, businesses can identify winning combinations that optimize conversions. Ongoing experimentation enables businesses to continuously refine their website and marketing strategies.

6. Personalization and Targeted Messaging:

Personalization is a powerful tactic in CRO. By tailoring messaging, offers, and content based on user preferences, demographics, or browsing history, businesses can create a more relevant and engaging experience. Personalized recommendations, dynamic content, and targeted campaigns increase the chances of conversions by delivering precisely what users are looking for.

7. Optimizing Landing Pages:

Landing pages are critical elements in the conversion funnel. Optimizing landing pages involves aligning them with specific marketing campaigns, ensuring clear and compelling messaging, utilizing persuasive design elements, and incorporating strong calls-to-action. Well-designed landing pages maximize the chances of conversions by providing a focused and persuasive user experience.

8. Continuous Monitoring and Iteration:

CRO is an ongoing process that requires continuous monitoring and iteration. By regularly tracking and analyzing key metrics, businesses can identify areas for improvement, test new strategies, and refine their conversion optimization efforts. Regular performance reviews and data analysis allow businesses to adapt to changing user behaviors and optimize their website and marketing strategies accordingly.

Conclusion:

Conversion rate optimization is a powerful strategy that enables businesses to extract the maximum value from their website traffic. By setting clear goals, conducting data analysis, optimizing user experience, and implementing A/B testing, businesses can continuously improve their website and marketing campaigns to enhance conversions. Personalization, optimized landing pages, and continuous monitoring and iteration further contribute to CRO success. By embracing CRO as an integral part of their digital marketing strategy, businesses can unlock the full potential of their website, increase conversions, and drive meaningful results in an increasingly competitive online landscape.

3. Search Engine Optimization (SEO)

SEO boosts website visibility in search results, driving organic traffic by optimizing content, keywords, and building backlinks.

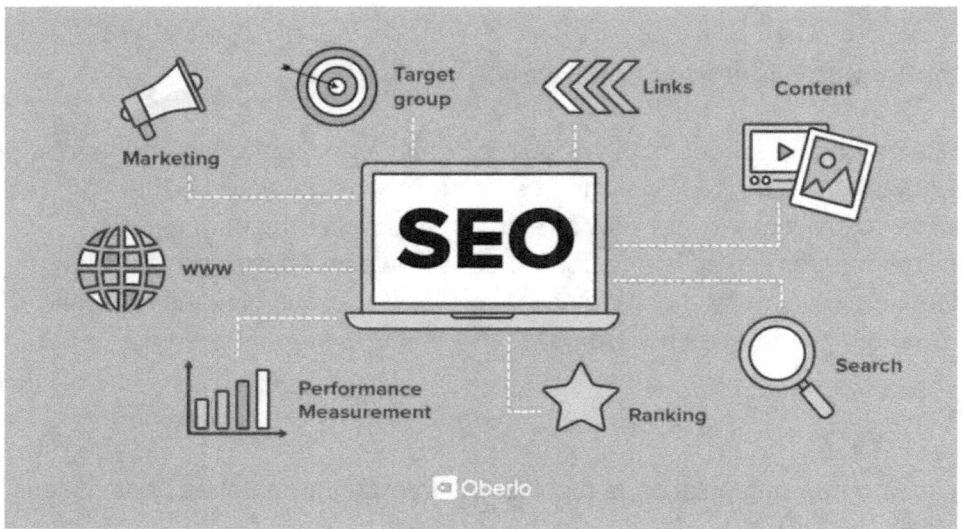

3.1 Fundamentals of SEO

Navigating the Digital Landscape: The Fundamentals of SEO

Introduction:

In the ever-expanding digital world, Search Engine Optimization (SEO) has become a cornerstone for businesses seeking to enhance their online visibility, attract organic traffic, and improve their search engine rankings. SEO involves optimizing websites to align with search engine algorithms and provide the most relevant and valuable content to users. In this article, we will explore the fundamental principles and best practices of SEO to help businesses navigate the intricacies of this essential digital marketing strategy.

1. Understanding Search Engine Optimization:

Search Engine Optimization is the practice of optimizing websites to improve their visibility and ranking in search engine results pages (SERPs). SEO involves a combination of technical optimizations, on-page optimizations, off-page optimizations, and content strategies. The goal is to increase organic (non-paid) traffic and drive relevant users to a website.

2. Keyword Research and Targeting:

Keyword research is a foundational step in SEO. It involves identifying the keywords and phrases that users are searching for related to a business's products or services. By targeting relevant keywords with high search volume and low competition, businesses can optimize their website content to appear prominently in search results.

3. On-Page Optimization:

On-page optimization focuses on optimizing individual web pages to improve their visibility and relevance. This includes optimizing meta tags (title tags, meta descriptions), URL structures, header tags, and incorporating targeted keywords naturally throughout the content. On-page optimization also involves improving website loading speed, mobile-friendliness, and user experience.

4. Technical SEO:

Technical SEO refers to the optimization of the website's technical aspects to ensure search engines can crawl, index, and understand the content effectively. This includes optimizing website architecture, XML sitemaps, canonical tags, robots.txt file, and resolving issues related to crawl errors, duplicate content, broken links, and website accessibility.

5. Off-Page Optimization and Link Building:

Off-page optimization focuses on building a strong backlink profile and improving the website's authority and credibility. This involves acquiring high-quality backlinks from reputable websites, engaging in guest blogging, social media promotion, and building relationships with influencers or industry experts. Quality backlinks signal to search engines that the website is trustworthy and authoritative.

6. Content Strategy and Optimization:

Content is a crucial component of SEO. Creating high-quality, relevant, and engaging content helps attract and retain users, encourages social sharing, and earns backlinks. Content optimization involves conducting keyword research, creating informative and compelling content, incorporating relevant keywords, and ensuring readability and proper formatting.

7. User Experience and Mobile Optimization:

User experience (UX) and mobile optimization are integral to SEO. Search engines prioritize websites that provide a positive user experience, including fast loading times, intuitive navigation, mobile-friendliness, and responsive design. Optimizing for mobile devices is particularly important, given the increasing use of smartphones and the emphasis search engines place on mobile-friendly websites.

8. Monitoring, Analytics, and Continuous Improvement:

SEO is an ongoing process that requires monitoring, analysis, and continuous improvement. Using tools like Google Analytics and Search Console, businesses can track website traffic, keyword rankings, user behavior, and engagement metrics. This data provides insights into the effectiveness of SEO efforts and enables businesses to make data-driven decisions and refine their strategies.

Conclusion:

Search Engine Optimization is a dynamic and essential aspect of digital marketing. By understanding the fundamentals of SEO, businesses can improve their online visibility, attract organic traffic, and connect with their target audience effectively. Keyword research, on-page optimization, technical SEO, off-page optimization, content strategy, user experience, and continuous monitoring are all key components of a successful SEO strategy. Embracing SEO as a long-term investment allows businesses to stay ahead in the competitive digital landscape, drive sustainable organic traffic, and achieve their goals. By prioritizing SEO best practices and adapting to evolving search engine algorithms, businesses can unlock the potential of their website and maximize their online presence.

3.2 Keyword Research and Analysis

Unveiling the Power of Keywords: A Comprehensive Guide to Keyword Research and Analysis

Introduction:

In the digital realm, keywords serve as the building blocks of search engine optimization (SEO) and pay-per-click (PPC) advertising campaigns. Keyword research and analysis play a pivotal role in understanding user intent, driving organic traffic, and optimizing website content. In this article, we will explore the importance of keyword research, the process of conducting keyword research, and how to analyze and leverage keywords effectively to enhance online visibility and reach the target audience.

1. The Significance of Keyword Research:

Keyword research is the foundation of SEO and PPC campaigns. It involves identifying the specific words and phrases that users enter into search engines when looking for information, products, or services. By understanding user intent and behavior, businesses can optimize their website content and PPC campaigns to align with relevant keywords, attracting targeted traffic and increasing the chances of conversions.

2. Establishing Goals and Target Audience:

Before diving into keyword research, businesses must define their goals and understand their target audience. Clearly defined goals help determine the desired outcomes of SEO and PPC efforts, such as increasing sales, generating leads, or improving brand awareness. Understanding the target audience's demographics, preferences, and search behavior aids in identifying the most relevant keywords to target.

3. Brainstorming and Generating Keyword Ideas:

Brainstorming is an essential starting point for keyword research. Begin by brainstorming a list of potential keywords related to the business, products, or services. Consider the main categories, subcategories, and variations of keywords that users might use when searching. Utilize keyword suggestion tools, competitor analysis, and customer feedback to expand the list further.

4. Utilizing Keyword Research Tools:

Keyword research tools are invaluable resources for uncovering keyword opportunities. Tools like Google Keyword Planner, SEMrush, Moz Keyword Explorer, and Ahrefs provide insights into keyword search volume, competition, trends, and related keywords. Utilize these tools to refine and expand the initial list of keywords, identifying the most relevant and valuable ones.

5. Analyzing Keyword Relevance and Competition:

Keyword relevance and competition analysis are crucial steps in keyword research. Assess the relevance of each keyword to the business and its target audience. Consider the search intent behind the keywords and their alignment with the website's content. Evaluate the level of competition for each keyword, considering factors such as organic competition, paid advertising competition, and search engine result pages (SERPs) analysis.

6. Long-Tail Keywords and Intent-Based Keywords:

Long-tail keywords and intent-based keywords are essential considerations in keyword research. Long-tail keywords are longer, more specific phrases that typically have lower search volume but higher conversion potential.

Intent-based keywords focus on understanding the user's search intent, such as informational, navigational, or transactional intent. Incorporating a mix of long-tail and intent-based keywords provides a well-rounded approach to keyword targeting.

7. Mapping Keywords to Website Content:

Once a list of relevant keywords is established, it's essential to map them to specific website pages or content. Identify the most suitable landing pages or create new content that aligns with each keyword's intent. Optimize the page's title tags, meta descriptions, headers, and body content to incorporate the targeted keywords naturally and provide valuable information to users.

8. Monitoring, Tracking, and Refining:

Keyword research is an iterative process that requires continuous monitoring, tracking, and refinement. Regularly analyze website analytics, search engine rankings, and user behavior data to evaluate the performance of targeted keywords. Identify opportunities to improve content, identify new keyword trends, and refine the keyword targeting strategy based on data-driven insights.

Conclusion:

Keyword research and analysis are vital components of a successful SEO and PPC strategy. By understanding user intent, identifying relevant keywords, and mapping them to website content, businesses can attract targeted organic traffic, improve search engine rankings, and drive conversions. Utilize keyword research tools, analyze keyword relevance and competition, and stay up-to-date with keyword trends to ensure the ongoing effectiveness of keyword targeting. Remember that keyword research is an iterative process that requires monitoring, tracking, and refinement. By continually optimizing website content and adapting keyword strategies based on data-driven insights, businesses can unlock the power of keywords and maximize their online visibility in the competitive digital landscape.

2.3 On-Page Optimization Techniques

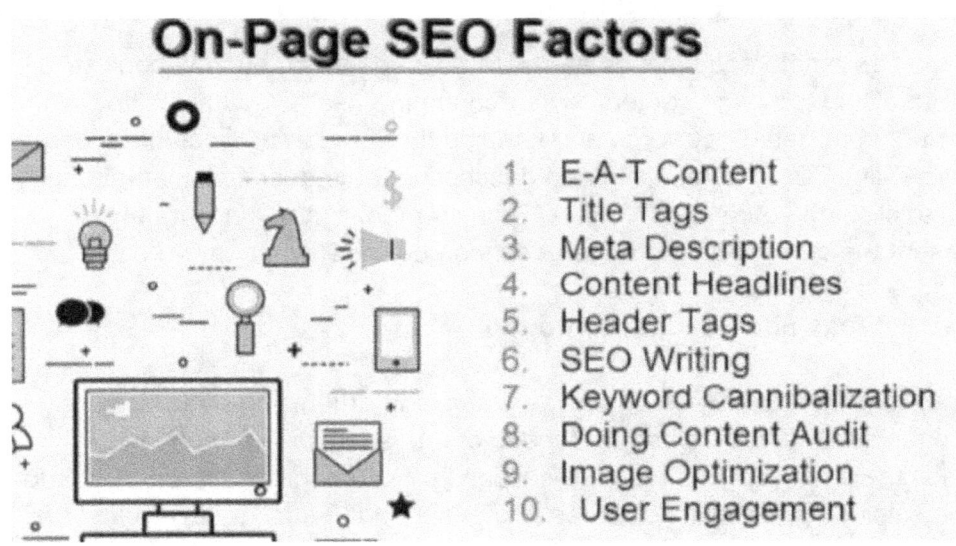

Elevating Your Website: On-Page Optimization Techniques for Improved Performance

Introduction:

On-page optimization is a crucial aspect of search engine optimization (SEO) that focuses on optimizing individual web pages to improve their visibility, relevance, and overall performance. By implementing on-page optimization techniques, businesses can enhance user experience, attract organic traffic, and achieve higher search engine rankings. In this article, we will explore the key on-page optimization techniques and best practices that can elevate your website's performance and drive meaningful results.

1. Keyword Optimization:

Keyword optimization is at the core of on-page optimization. It involves incorporating relevant keywords naturally into various on-page elements, including titles, headings, meta tags, URLs, and body content. Conduct thorough keyword research to identify the most valuable and relevant keywords for your web pages. Ensure that keywords are strategically placed, but avoid keyword stuffing, which can have a negative impact on both user experience and search engine rankings.

2. Title Tags and Meta Descriptions:

Title tags and meta descriptions are HTML elements that provide concise summaries of web page content to search engine users. Optimize title tags by including targeted keywords and keeping them within the recommended character limit. Craft compelling and descriptive meta descriptions that entice users to click on your search results. Both elements should accurately represent the content on the page and incorporate relevant keywords.

3. Header Tags and Heading Structure:

Header tags (H1, H2, H3, etc.) play a vital role in organizing and structuring web page content. Utilize header tags to create a logical hierarchy that outlines the main sections and sub-sections of your content. Optimize header tags by including relevant keywords and ensuring they accurately reflect the content beneath them. Proper heading structure enhances readability, improves user experience, and signals the importance of the content to search engines.

4. URL Structure:

URL structure impacts both user experience and search engine optimization. Create clean, concise, and descriptive URLs that include relevant keywords and accurately represent the page's content. Avoid using generic or confusing URLs with numbers or excessive parameters. Utilize hyphens to separate words within the URL, making it easier for users and search engines to understand.

5. Image Optimization:

Images are an integral part of web pages, but they can impact page load times if not optimized properly. Compress images to reduce file size without compromising quality. Use descriptive file names and include relevant alt tags that accurately describe the image content. Alt tags are important for accessibility and help search engines understand the context of the images.

6. Content Optimization:

High-quality and relevant content is essential for on-page optimization. Create original, informative, and engaging content that provides value to users. Incorporate targeted keywords naturally within the content, but prioritize user experience and readability. Use subheadings, bullet points, and formatting to improve content structure and organization. Aim for comprehensive and authoritative content that addresses user queries and provides in-depth information.

7. Internal Linking:

Internal linking refers to linking to other pages within your website. It helps search engines discover and crawl pages more effectively, improves website navigation, and distributes link equity. Incorporate relevant anchor text when linking to other pages, using descriptive and keyword-rich phrases. Consider the user journey and strategically place internal links to guide users to relevant and related content.

8. User Experience Optimization:

User experience is a critical factor in on-page optimization. Ensure that your web pages are user-friendly, visually appealing, and optimized for various devices. Optimize page load times by compressing images, leveraging caching, and minimizing unnecessary scripts. Improve website navigation and ensure easy access to important information. Prioritize responsive design to provide a seamless experience across desktop, mobile, and tablet devices.

9. Social Sharing Integration:

Social sharing integration encourages users to share your content on various social media platforms. Incorporate social sharing buttons that allow users to easily share your web pages or blog posts. This can increase visibility, attract more traffic, and potentially improve search engine rankings through social signals.

10. Continuous Monitoring and Improvement:

On-page optimization is an ongoing process that requires continuous monitoring and improvement. Regularly analyze website analytics, user behavior, and search engine rankings to identify areas for improvement. Utilize tools like Google Analytics and Search Console to track page performance, keyword rankings, and user engagement metrics. Based on data-driven insights, refine your on-page optimization strategies and make necessary adjustments to improve performance.

Conclusion:

On-page optimization techniques are essential for improving website visibility, relevance, and overall performance. By implementing keyword optimization, optimizing title tags and meta descriptions, utilizing header tags and structured URLs, optimizing images and content, and enhancing user experience, businesses can elevate their website's performance in search engine rankings. Incorporating internal linking, social sharing integration, and continuously monitoring and improving on-page elements ensure that your website remains competitive and delivers an exceptional user experience. By prioritizing on-page optimization and staying up-to-date with industry best practices, businesses can attract organic traffic, engage users, and achieve their SEO goals in the dynamic digital landscape.

3.4 Off-Page Optimization Strategies

On Page vs. Off Page vs. Technical SEO

On Page SEO	Off Page SEO	Technical SEO
Site content	Link Building	Site speed
Title tag and meta tag optimization	Content marketing	Structured data
	Social media	Canonicalization
H tag optimization	Podcasts	XML Sitemaps
Internal linking	Reviews	Hreflang
Image optimization	and more	and more

Expanding Your Reach: Effective Off-Page Optimization Strategies

Introduction:

Off-page optimization is a critical component of search engine optimization (SEO) that focuses on improving a website's visibility and authority beyond its own pages. By implementing off-page optimization strategies, businesses can enhance their online reputation, attract quality backlinks, and improve search engine rankings. In this article, we will explore key off-page optimization strategies and best practices that can expand your website's reach and drive meaningful results.

1. Building High-Quality Backlinks:

Building high-quality backlinks is one of the most influential off-page optimization strategies. Backlinks serve as votes of confidence from other websites, signaling to search engines the relevance and authority of your website. Focus on acquiring backlinks from reputable and relevant sources through guest blogging, influencer partnerships, content promotion, and participation in industry forums and communities.

2. Social Media Engagement:

Social media engagement plays a crucial role in off-page optimization. Establish a strong presence on relevant social media platforms, engage with your audience, and share valuable content. Encourage social sharing and participation, as social signals can indirectly influence search engine rankings. Actively participate in discussions, respond to comments, and share relevant industry news to build brand visibility and attract potential backlinks.

3. Online Reputation Management:

Maintaining a positive online reputation is vital for off-page optimization. Monitor and manage online reviews, ratings, and mentions of your brand. Address customer feedback and resolve issues promptly to demonstrate your commitment to customer satisfaction. A positive online reputation not only enhances your brand's credibility but also encourages other websites to link to your content.

4. Influencer Marketing and Outreach:

Influencer marketing and outreach can significantly impact off-page optimization. Identify influential individuals in your industry and build relationships with them. Collaborate on content creation, guest blogging, or joint promotions to leverage their audience and attract quality backlinks. Influencers can amplify your brand's reach and provide valuable endorsements that enhance your website's authority.

5. Guest Blogging and Content Contributions:

Guest blogging and content contributions are effective ways to build backlinks and expand your online presence. Identify authoritative blogs and publications in your industry and offer to contribute valuable content. Ensure that your guest posts provide unique insights and deliver value to the readers. Incorporate relevant backlinks to your website within the content or author bio to drive traffic and enhance visibility.

6. Online Directories and Listings:

Submit your website to reputable online directories and listings relevant to your industry or location. This can improve your website's visibility in search engine results and attract potential backlinks. Ensure that your business information is consistent and up to date across directories, as search engines consider the consistency of information when determining your website's credibility.

7. Brand Mentions and Link Reclamation:

Monitor online mentions of your brand and website, even if they do not include a direct backlink. Reach out to websites that mention your brand without linking and request a backlink. Additionally, identify broken or redirected backlinks to your website and reach out to the website owner to request a correction or replacement link. This tactic can help reclaim lost link opportunities and boost your website's authority.

8. Online Forums and Communities:

Active participation in relevant online forums and communities can contribute to off-page optimization. Engage in discussions, provide valuable insights, and answer questions related to your industry or niche. By establishing yourself as a knowledgeable and trustworthy contributor, you can attract attention, gain visibility, and potentially earn backlinks from other forum members or website owners.

9. Press Releases and Media Outreach:

Publishing press releases and engaging in media outreach can enhance off-page optimization efforts. Announce newsworthy events, product launches, or industry insights through press releases distributed to relevant media outlets. Build relationships with journalists and influencers in your industry and pitch story ideas or provide expert insights for media coverage. Media mentions and backlinks from reputable sources can significantly boost your website's visibility and authority.

10. Continuous Monitoring and Analysis:

Off-page optimization requires continuous monitoring and analysis. Utilize tools like Google Analytics, backlink analysis tools, and social media monitoring tools to track website traffic, backlink profiles, social engagement, and brand mentions. Analyze the effectiveness of your off-page strategies, identify areas for improvement, and adapt your approach based on data-driven insights.

Conclusion:

Off-page optimization is essential for expanding your website's reach, authority, and visibility. By implementing effective off-page optimization strategies such as building high-quality backlinks, engaging on social media, managing your online reputation, and utilizing influencer marketing and outreach, you can enhance your website's SEO performance. Guest blogging, online directory listings, and active participation in online forums and communities contribute to increased visibility and backlink acquisition. Additionally, press releases, media outreach, and continuous monitoring and analysis ensure that your off-page optimization efforts are refined and yield meaningful results. By adopting a comprehensive approach to off-page optimization, businesses can strengthen their online presence, attract relevant traffic, and improve their search engine rankings in the competitive digital landscape.

3.5 SEO Tools and Analytics

Unleashing the Power of SEO Tools and Analytics for Data-Driven Success

Introduction:

In the dynamic realm of search engine optimization (SEO), utilizing the right tools and analytics is crucial for optimizing website performance, gaining insights, and making data-driven decisions. SEO tools and analytics provide valuable information about website traffic, keyword rankings, backlinks, user behavior, and more. In this article, we will explore the essential SEO tools and analytics that can empower businesses to maximize their SEO efforts and achieve measurable success.

1. Keyword Research Tools:

Keyword research tools, such as Google Keyword Planner, SEMrush, and Moz Keyword Explorer, help identify relevant keywords and provide insights into search volume, competition, and trends. These tools assist in finding valuable keyword opportunities, understanding user intent, and refining keyword targeting strategies.

2. Website Analytics Platforms:

Website analytics platforms, like Google Analytics, offer comprehensive data on website performance, user behavior, traffic sources, conversion rates, and more. By analyzing this data, businesses can gain insights into website traffic patterns, identify areas for improvement, and track the effectiveness of SEO strategies.

3. Rank Tracking Tools:

Rank tracking tools, such as Ahrefs, SEMrush, and Moz, enable businesses to monitor keyword rankings in search engine results pages (SERPs). These tools provide valuable information about keyword positions, visibility, and fluctuations, allowing businesses to track progress, identify opportunities, and refine their SEO strategies accordingly.

4. Backlink Analysis Tools:

Backlink analysis tools, such as Ahrefs, Majestic, and SEMrush, help businesses monitor and analyze their backlink profiles. These tools provide insights into the quantity, quality, and diversity of backlinks pointing to a website. Backlink analysis helps businesses identify potential link building opportunities, assess competitor strategies, and enhance their website's authority.

5. On-Page Optimization Tools:

On-page optimization tools, such as Yoast SEO, Moz On-Page Grader, and SEMrush On-Page SEO Checker, assist in optimizing individual web pages. These tools analyze on-page elements, such as title tags, meta descriptions, headings, and content, providing suggestions for improvement to enhance search engine visibility and user experience.

6. Technical SEO Tools:

Technical SEO tools, like Google Search Console and Screaming Frog, help identify and resolve technical issues that impact website performance. These tools crawl websites, analyze metadata, identify broken links, detect crawl errors, and provide recommendations for optimization. Technical SEO tools ensure websites are crawlable, indexable, and free from technical barriers.

7. Social Media Analytics:

Social media analytics platforms, such as Facebook Insights, Twitter Analytics, and Instagram Insights, provide valuable data on social media engagement, audience demographics, reach, and impressions. By understanding social media performance, businesses can optimize social media strategies, identify content opportunities, and improve brand visibility.

8. Competitor Analysis Tools:

Competitor analysis tools, like SEMrush, SpyFu, and SimilarWeb, help businesses gain insights into their competitors' strategies, keywords, traffic sources, and backlinks. By analyzing competitor data, businesses can identify opportunities, benchmark their performance, and refine their SEO strategies to stay competitive in the market.

9. User Experience Testing Tools:

User experience testing tools, such as Hotjar, Crazy Egg, and Optimizely, enable businesses to conduct heatmaps, user recordings, A/B testing, and user surveys. These tools provide valuable insights into user behavior, engagement, and conversion rates. By analyzing user experience data, businesses can optimize website design, navigation, and conversion funnels to enhance user satisfaction.

10. Continuous Monitoring and Reporting:

Continuous monitoring and reporting tools, like Google Data Studio and SEMrush Sensor, help businesses track and report on key SEO metrics and performance indicators. These tools enable businesses to create customized reports, track progress, and communicate results effectively to stakeholders.

Conclusion:

SEO tools and analytics are invaluable assets for businesses seeking to optimize their website's performance and drive data-driven success. Keyword research tools, website analytics platforms, and rank tracking tools provide insights into user behavior, keyword performance, and website visibility. Backlink analysis tools, on-page optimization tools, and technical SEO tools assist in improving website authority, user experience, and search engine visibility. Social media analytics, competitor analysis tools, and user experience testing tools provide additional layers of data to inform strategies and benchmark performance. Continuous monitoring and reporting tools help businesses track progress, communicate results, and refine SEO strategies over time. By leveraging the power of SEO tools and analytics, businesses can gain a competitive edge, make informed decisions, and achieve measurable success in the ever-evolving landscape of SEO.

4. Pay-Per-Click (PPC) Advertising

PPC advertising: Businesses pay for each click on their ads, targeting audiences, increasing brand visibility, and driving website traffic through strategically placed paid ads.

4.1 Introduction to PPC Advertising

Exploring the Possibilities: An Introduction to PPC Advertising

Introduction:

Pay-per-click (PPC) advertising has revolutionized the digital marketing landscape, offering businesses a powerful tool to drive targeted traffic, increase brand visibility, and achieve specific marketing goals. PPC advertising allows businesses to display ads on search engines and other platforms, paying only when a user clicks on the ad. In this article, we will provide a comprehensive introduction to PPC advertising, exploring its benefits, key components, and best practices to help businesses harness its potential and maximize their online success.

1. Understanding PPC Advertising:

PPC advertising is an online advertising model where advertisers pay a fee each time their ad is clicked. It is a form of paid advertising that allows businesses to bid for ad placement on search engines, social media platforms, and other relevant websites. PPC offers immediate visibility and control over ad spend, making it a popular choice for businesses looking for quick results and measurable returns on investment (ROI).

2. Benefits of PPC Advertising:

PPC advertising offers numerous benefits for businesses. It provides instant visibility and exposure to targeted audiences, driving immediate traffic to websites. PPC allows for precise targeting, ensuring ads are shown to users who are actively searching for relevant products or services. With PPC, businesses have control over budget allocation and can set maximum bids, ensuring cost control and ROI optimization. PPC campaigns also provide valuable data and insights that can be used to refine marketing strategies and improve campaign performance.

3. Key Components of PPC Advertising:

PPC advertising involves several key components. Keyword research is essential to identify relevant keywords that users search for when looking for products or services. Ad creation involves crafting compelling and relevant ad copy that attracts user attention. Ad targeting allows businesses to define their target audience based on demographics, location, interests, and more. Bid management determines how much an advertiser is willing to pay for each click, while ad extensions provide additional information or calls-to-action within ads to enhance their effectiveness.

4. Choosing the Right PPC Platform:

There are various PPC platforms available, each with its unique features and targeting options. Google Ads (formerly Google AdWords) is the most popular PPC platform, reaching a vast audience through its search network, display network, and YouTube. Social media platforms like Facebook Ads, Twitter Ads, and LinkedIn Ads offer advanced targeting capabilities to reach specific user demographics and interests. Other platforms, such as Bing Ads and Amazon Advertising, provide additional opportunities to target specific audiences and expand reach.

5. Setting Up a PPC Campaign:

Setting up a successful PPC campaign involves several key steps. It starts with defining campaign objectives and selecting the right PPC platform. Thorough keyword research helps identify relevant and high-performing keywords to target. Ad creation involves crafting compelling ad copy that aligns with campaign goals and resonates with the target audience. Ad targeting settings are configured to define the audience based on demographics, location, and interests. Budget allocation, bidding strategies, and tracking mechanisms are established to optimize ad spend and measure campaign performance.

6. Monitoring and Optimization:

Monitoring and optimizing PPC campaigns are crucial for achieving desired outcomes. Regularly review campaign performance metrics, such as click-through rates (CTR), conversion rates, and cost per acquisition (CPA), to identify areas for improvement. Refine keyword targeting, ad copy, and ad extensions based on data-driven insights. Continuously monitor bid prices and adjust bids to maintain cost-effectiveness. A/B testing allows businesses to test different ad variations and landing pages to optimize performance. Regularly analyze campaign data, make data-driven decisions, and optimize campaigns to achieve the best results.

7. Ad Quality and Relevance:

Ad quality and relevance are essential for successful PPC advertising. Ads should be compelling, concise, and tailored to the target audience. Ensure that the ad copy aligns with the landing page content to provide a seamless user experience. Utilize ad extensions to provide additional information or call-to-action to increase ad visibility and click-through rates. Optimize landing pages for relevance and user experience to maximize conversion rates and achieve campaign goals.

8. Tracking and Analytics:

Tracking and analytics are vital for measuring the effectiveness of PPC campaigns. Use conversion tracking to monitor and analyze the actions users take after clicking on ads, such as form submissions, purchases, or downloads. Implement tracking pixels or codes to capture valuable data and insights. Analytics platforms like Google Analytics provide in-depth data on website traffic, user behavior, and campaign performance. Leverage these insights to refine targeting, optimize bidding strategies, and improve overall campaign performance.

Conclusion:

PPC advertising offers businesses an effective and measurable way to drive targeted traffic, increase brand visibility, and achieve specific marketing objectives. By understanding the fundamentals of PPC advertising, including its benefits, key components, and best practices, businesses can leverage this powerful advertising model to maximize their online success. Thorough keyword research, compelling ad creation, precise ad targeting, and effective bid management are all crucial aspects of a successful PPC campaign. Monitoring campaign performance, optimizing ad quality and relevance, and utilizing tracking and analytics ensure continuous improvement and data-driven decision-making. By embracing PPC advertising as part of a comprehensive digital marketing strategy, businesses can reach their target audience, drive conversions, and achieve their desired goals in the competitive digital landscape.

4.2 Google Ads (Formerly AdWords)

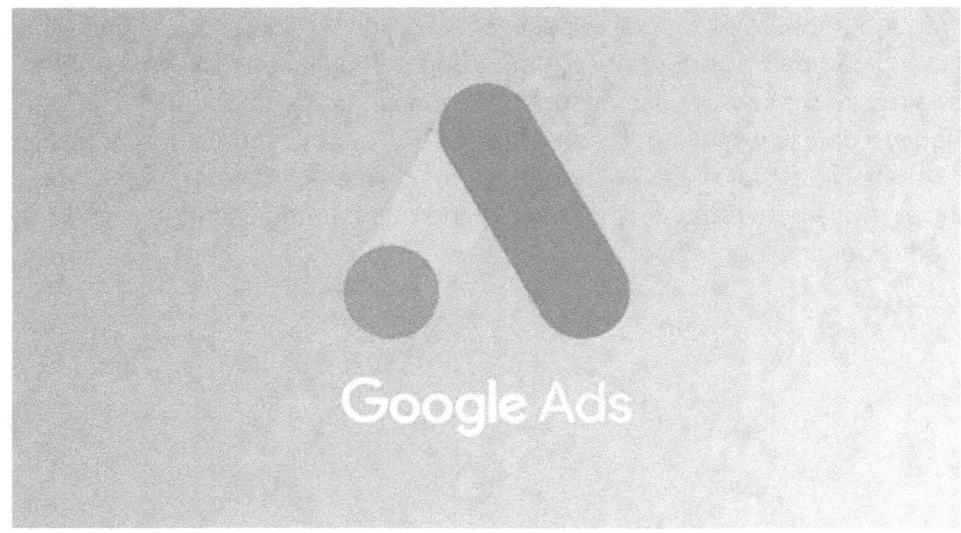

Google Ads (Formerly AdWords): Unleashing the Power of Online Advertising

Introduction:

Google Ads, formerly known as Google AdWords, is a powerful online advertising platform that allows businesses to reach their target audience, increase brand visibility, and drive relevant traffic to their websites. With its vast reach and advanced targeting capabilities, Google Ads has become an essential tool for businesses looking to maximize their online advertising efforts. In this article, we will explore the key features, benefits, and best practices of Google Ads, empowering businesses to harness its potential and achieve success in the digital advertising landscape.

1. Understanding Google Ads:

Google Ads is an online advertising platform developed by Google. It allows businesses to create and display ads across various Google-owned properties, including the search engine results page (SERP), display network, YouTube, and partner websites. Google Ads operates on a pay-per-click (PPC) model, where advertisers bid on keywords and pay only when their ads are clicked. This ensures that businesses have control over their advertising budget and can measure the return on investment (ROI) effectively.

2. Benefits of Google Ads:

Google Ads offers numerous benefits for businesses of all sizes. It provides access to a vast audience, as Google is the most popular search engine globally. With advanced targeting options, businesses can reach specific demographics, locations, and interests. Google Ads offers flexibility in budget allocation and bid management, allowing businesses to set maximum bids and daily budgets. The platform provides real-time data and insights, enabling advertisers to optimize campaigns based on performance metrics. Google Ads also offers various ad formats, including text ads, display ads, video ads, shopping ads, and app promotion ads, catering to diverse marketing goals.

3. Key Components of Google Ads:

Google Ads comprises several key components that advertisers should be familiar with. Campaigns are the highest-level structure, allowing advertisers to set specific objectives and budgets. Ad groups organize ads and keywords based on themes or product categories. Keywords are crucial for targeting relevant search queries and triggering ads. Ad creation involves crafting compelling ad copy that attracts users and generates clicks. Ad extensions provide additional information or call-to-action within ads to increase visibility and click-through rates. Quality Score is a metric that assesses the relevance and quality of ads, keywords, and landing pages, influencing ad rank and cost-per-click (CPC).

4. Setting Up a Google Ads Campaign:

Setting up a successful Google Ads campaign involves several steps. Start by defining campaign objectives and selecting the most relevant campaign type, such as search, display, video, shopping, or app promotion. Thorough keyword research helps identify relevant and high-performing keywords to target. Ad creation involves crafting compelling ad copy that aligns with campaign goals and resonates with the target audience. Ad targeting settings are configured to define the audience based on demographics, location, interests, and more. Budget allocation, bidding strategies, and ad scheduling are established to optimize ad spend and reach the target audience effectively.

5. Ad Rank and Quality Score:

Ad Rank determines the position of ads in the search engine results page (SERP) and considers factors such as bid amount, ad quality, and expected click-through rate (CTR). Quality Score is a critical component of Ad Rank and evaluates the relevance and quality of ads, keywords, and landing pages. To improve Ad Rank and Quality Score, businesses should focus on creating high-quality, relevant ad copy, optimizing landing pages, and ensuring strong keyword relevance.

6. Ad Extensions:

Ad extensions are additional pieces of information or call-to-action that enhance the effectiveness of ads. They provide more visibility, improve ad relevance, and increase click-through rates. Google Ads offers various ad extensions, including sitelink extensions, call extensions, location extensions, callout extensions, and structured snippet extensions. Ad extensions allow businesses to provide additional information, such as specific product offerings, contact details, or promotional messages, within their ads.

7. Conversion Tracking and Measurement:

Conversion tracking and measurement are vital for evaluating the effectiveness of Google Ads campaigns. Setting up conversion tracking allows businesses to monitor and analyze the actions users take after clicking on ads, such as form submissions, purchases, or sign-ups. Conversion tracking provides insights into campaign performance, return on ad spend (ROAS), and cost per acquisition (CPA). Google Analytics integration can further enhance tracking capabilities, providing in-depth data on website traffic, user behavior, and campaign performance.

8. Monitoring and Optimization:

Monitoring and optimizing Google Ads campaigns are crucial for achieving desired outcomes. Regularly review campaign performance metrics, such as click-through rates (CTR), conversion rates, and cost per conversion. Refine keyword targeting, ad copy, and ad extensions based on data-driven insights. Continuously monitor bid prices and adjust bids to maintain cost-effectiveness. A/B testing allows businesses to test different ad variations and landing pages to optimize performance. Regularly analyze campaign data, make data-driven decisions, and optimize campaigns to achieve the best results.

Conclusion:

Google Ads provides businesses with a powerful platform to reach their target audience, increase brand visibility, and drive relevant traffic to their websites. By understanding the key features, benefits, and best practices of Google Ads, businesses can optimize their online advertising efforts and achieve measurable success. Thorough campaign setup, effective keyword targeting, compelling ad copy, and strategic use of ad extensions are all crucial components of a successful Google Ads campaign. Monitoring campaign performance, refining ad quality, and leveraging conversion tracking and measurement ensure continuous improvement and data-driven decision-making. By harnessing the power of Google Ads, businesses can maximize their online advertising potential, drive conversions, and achieve their marketing goals in the ever-evolving digital landscape.

4.3 Bing Ads And Other PPC Platforms

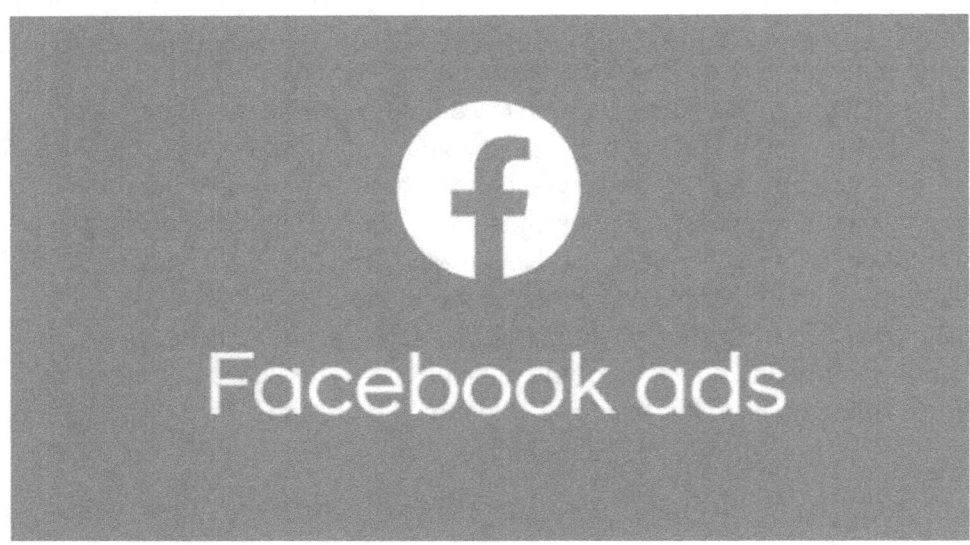

Beyond Google: Exploring Bing Ads and Other PPC Platforms

Introduction:

While Google Ads (formerly AdWords) is the dominant player in the pay-per-click (PPC) advertising landscape, there are other powerful PPC platforms that businesses can leverage to expand their reach and drive targeted traffic. Bing Ads, Facebook Ads, LinkedIn Ads, and Twitter Ads are among the notable platforms that offer unique features, targeting options, and audience reach. In this article, we will explore Bing Ads and other PPC platforms, highlighting their benefits, key components, and best practices. By understanding the diverse options available, businesses can diversify their advertising strategies and tap into untapped audiences to maximize their online advertising success.

1. Bing Ads: The Alternative to Google Ads:

Bing Ads is Microsoft's PPC advertising platform, serving ads on the Bing search engine and its network of partner sites, including Yahoo and AOL. While Google dominates the search engine market share, Bing still holds a significant portion, making Bing Ads an attractive option for businesses. Bing Ads offers similar features to Google Ads, including keyword targeting, ad creation, bid management, and conversion tracking. It provides an opportunity to reach a different user demographic and tap into less competitive markets. Bing Ads often has lower cost-per-click (CPC) rates than Google Ads, potentially resulting in a more cost-effective advertising strategy.

2. Facebook Ads: Targeted Advertising on the Social Media Giant:

Facebook Ads is a leading social media advertising platform, allowing businesses to reach over two billion active users. With advanced targeting options based on demographics, interests, behaviors, and connections, Facebook Ads provides a unique opportunity to engage with highly relevant audiences. It offers various ad formats, including image ads, video ads, carousel ads, and lead generation ads. Facebook's extensive user data allows for precise audience targeting and retargeting, making it a valuable platform for businesses looking to drive engagement, conversions, and brand awareness.

3. LinkedIn Ads: Targeting Professionals and B2B Audiences:

LinkedIn Ads caters specifically to professionals and businesses, making it a powerful platform for B2B advertising. With over 740 million members, LinkedIn provides access to a vast network of professionals, allowing businesses to target specific industries, job titles, company sizes, and more. LinkedIn Ads offer various ad formats, including sponsored content, text ads, and dynamic ads. It also provides robust targeting options for precise audience segmentation and the ability to engage with decision-makers and influencers in the professional world.

4. Twitter Ads: Real-Time Engagement and Brand Awareness:

Twitter Ads enables businesses to promote their products, services, and content on the popular social media platform. With over 330 million active users, Twitter offers a real-time engagement opportunity and the ability to reach a global audience. Twitter Ads provides various ad formats, including promoted tweets, promoted accounts, and promoted trends. Targeting options allow businesses to reach specific demographics, interests, followers of relevant accounts, and keywords. Twitter Ads can be effective for driving brand awareness, engagement, and conversations around a specific topic or event.

5. Amazon Advertising: Targeting Shoppers on the E-commerce Giant:

Amazon Advertising offers businesses the opportunity to reach millions of shoppers on the e-commerce giant's platform. With advanced targeting options based on customer search behavior, product interests, and shopping history, businesses can showcase their products and drive sales directly on Amazon. Amazon Advertising offers various ad formats, including sponsored product ads, sponsored brand ads, and display ads. It provides robust analytics and conversion tracking to measure the effectiveness of advertising campaigns and optimize performance. Amazon Advertising is particularly beneficial for businesses operating in the e-commerce space, looking to maximize visibility and sales on the world's largest online marketplace.

6. Key Components of PPC Platforms:

While each PPC platform has its unique features, they share common key components. These include campaign creation, keyword research and targeting, ad creation, bid management, and tracking and analytics. Businesses should thoroughly research and understand the nuances of each platform to create effective campaigns. Targeting options, ad formats, and bidding strategies may vary across platforms, necessitating a tailored approach to each PPC platform.

7. Best Practices for PPC Platforms:

Best practices for PPC platforms include thorough keyword research, crafting compelling ad copy, and aligning ad content with landing pages. Ad targeting should be precise, considering relevant demographics, interests, and behaviors. Monitoring campaign performance regularly and making data-driven decisions to optimize bids, budgets, and ad content are essential. A/B testing enables businesses to experiment with different ad variations to identify what resonates with the target audience. Conversion tracking and analytics should be implemented to measure ROI and make informed decisions. Keeping up with platform updates, exploring new features, and staying informed about audience trends and behavior ensure ongoing success with PPC advertising.

Conclusion:

While Google Ads remains the dominant PPC advertising platform, businesses should not overlook the opportunities offered by other platforms such as Bing Ads, Facebook Ads, LinkedIn Ads, Twitter Ads, and Amazon Advertising. These platforms provide unique features, targeting options, and audience reach that can help businesses expand their advertising strategies and tap into untapped markets. By understanding the key components and best practices of each platform, businesses can tailor their campaigns effectively, reach their target audience, and achieve measurable success. Diversifying advertising efforts across multiple PPC platforms allows businesses to maximize their online visibility, engage with relevant audiences, and drive conversions in the ever-evolving digital landscape.

4.4 Creating Effective PPC Campaigns

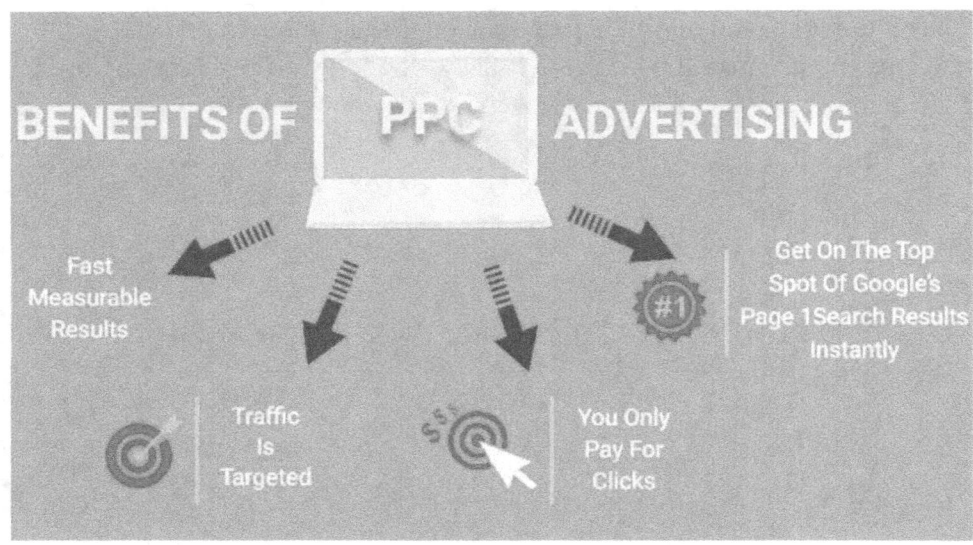

Creating Effective PPC Campaigns: Strategies for Maximizing Online Advertising Success

Introduction:

Pay-per-click (PPC) advertising is a powerful tool for businesses to drive targeted traffic, increase brand visibility, and achieve specific marketing goals. However, creating effective PPC campaigns requires careful planning, strategic execution, and continuous optimization. In this article, we will explore key strategies and best practices for creating successful PPC campaigns. From setting campaign objectives and conducting thorough keyword research to crafting compelling ad copy and optimizing landing pages, these strategies will empower businesses to maximize their online advertising success and generate measurable results.

1. Define Campaign Objectives:

Before launching a PPC campaign, it is crucial to clearly define campaign objectives. Determine what you aim to achieve, whether it's driving website traffic, generating leads, increasing sales, or raising brand awareness. Clear objectives help guide campaign setup and optimization efforts.

2. Thorough Keyword Research:

Thorough keyword research is essential for targeting the right audience and maximizing campaign performance. Utilize keyword research tools to identify relevant and high-performing keywords. Consider user intent, search volume, competition, and long-tail keywords to refine keyword targeting.

3. Crafting Compelling Ad Copy:

Crafting compelling ad copy is key to capturing user attention and driving clicks. Create concise, engaging, and relevant ad headlines and descriptions. Incorporate targeted keywords, highlight unique selling points, and include a clear call-to-action (CTA) to encourage user engagement.

4. Landing Page Optimization:

Optimizing landing pages is crucial for increasing conversion rates and achieving campaign objectives. Align landing page content with ad messaging, ensuring a seamless user experience. Optimize page load times, simplify navigation, and make the desired action clear. Implement clear and persuasive CTAs to drive conversions.

5. Ad Targeting and Segmentation:

Effective ad targeting and segmentation ensure ads reach the right audience. Leverage targeting options based on demographics, location, interests, and behaviors to refine audience targeting. Segment campaigns to tailor messaging and budgets based on audience characteristics.

6. Budget Allocation and Bid Management:

Strategically allocate campaign budgets and manage bids to maximize ROI. Set daily and campaign-level budgets based on campaign objectives. Continuously monitor performance metrics such as click-through rates (CTR), conversion rates, and cost per acquisition (CPA) to adjust bids for optimal performance.

7. Ad Testing and Optimization:

A/B testing allows businesses to experiment with different ad variations to identify what resonates with the target audience. Test different headlines, ad descriptions, calls-to-action, and visuals to optimize performance. Continuously monitor and analyze ad performance, making data-driven decisions to improve campaign effectiveness.

8. Conversion Tracking and Analytics:

Implement conversion tracking and analytics to measure campaign success and optimize performance. Set up conversion tracking to monitor key actions such as form submissions, purchases, or sign-ups. Leverage analytics platforms to track website traffic, user behavior, and campaign performance. Analyze data to identify trends, optimize targeting, and refine ad messaging.

9. Regular Monitoring and Optimization:

Regularly monitor campaign performance and make data-driven optimizations. Continuously review performance metrics such as CTR, conversion rates, and CPA. Adjust bids, refine targeting, and update ad copy based on performance insights. Stay updated with industry trends and platform updates to adapt campaigns accordingly.

10. Continuous Testing and Iteration:

PPC campaigns require continuous testing and iteration for ongoing success. Experiment with new keywords, ad variations, landing page designs, and targeting options to discover opportunities for improvement. Monitor competitor strategies and adapt campaigns to remain competitive.

Conclusion:

Creating effective PPC campaigns requires a strategic approach and ongoing optimization. By defining clear campaign objectives, conducting thorough keyword research, crafting compelling ad copy, and optimizing landing pages, businesses can drive targeted traffic and increase conversions. Ad targeting, budget allocation, and bid management should be aligned with campaign goals to maximize ROI. A/B testing enables businesses to optimize ad variations, while conversion tracking and analytics provide valuable insights for campaign optimization. Regular monitoring, data-driven decision-making, and continuous testing ensure that campaigns remain effective and adaptive to changing market dynamics. By implementing these strategies and best practices, businesses can create highly successful PPC campaigns, reach their target audience, and achieve their desired marketing objectives in the competitive digital landscape.

4.5 PPC Analytics and Optimization

Harnessing the Power of PPC Analytics and Optimization for Maximum Campaign Success

Introduction:

PPC advertising is a dynamic and data-driven marketing strategy that requires continuous monitoring, analysis, and optimization to maximize campaign success. By leveraging PPC analytics and implementing effective optimization techniques, businesses can refine their campaigns, improve performance, and achieve their marketing objectives. In this article, we will explore the importance of PPC analytics, key metrics to track, and optimization strategies that empower businesses to make data-driven decisions, optimize their campaigns, and drive maximum return on investment (ROI).

1. The Importance of PPC Analytics:

PPC analytics provide valuable insights into campaign performance, user behavior, and conversion tracking. By analyzing PPC data, businesses can understand their audience, identify trends, measure campaign effectiveness, and make informed decisions for optimization. PPC analytics enable businesses to track key metrics, optimize targeting, refine ad copy, and allocate budgets effectively.

2. Key Metrics to Track in PPC Campaigns:

Tracking and analyzing key metrics is vital for evaluating campaign success and optimizing performance. Metrics such as click-through rate (CTR), conversion rate, cost per click (CPC), cost per acquisition (CPA), return on ad spend (ROAS), and quality score provide valuable insights into the effectiveness of ad campaigns, keyword performance, and overall ROI.

3. Conversion Tracking and Attribution Modeling:

Implementing conversion tracking allows businesses to measure specific actions taken by users after clicking on ads, such as form submissions, purchases, or downloads. Attribution modeling helps businesses understand the touchpoints in a customer's journey that lead to conversions. By tracking conversions and utilizing attribution modeling, businesses can optimize their campaigns and allocate budgets more effectively.

4. A/B Testing and Ad Variation Optimization:

A/B testing is a powerful technique that allows businesses to experiment with different ad variations to identify the most effective ones. By testing different headlines, ad copy, calls-to-action, and visuals, businesses can optimize their campaigns based on data-driven insights. A/B testing helps improve click-through rates, conversion rates, and overall campaign performance.

5. Bid Management and Budget Optimization:

Optimizing bids and budget allocation is crucial for maximizing ROI and campaign success. Businesses should regularly analyze bid performance, adjust bids based on keyword performance and competition, and allocate budgets strategically to top-performing campaigns, ad groups, or keywords Implementing bid management techniques such as automated bidding strategies and bid adjustments helps optimize campaign performance.

6. Keyword Optimization and Expansion:

Keyword optimization and expansion involve continuously monitoring and refining keyword performance. Analyze keyword data, identify high-performing keywords, and optimize bidding strategies accordingly. Expand keyword lists by researching new relevant keywords and incorporating them into campaigns to reach a broader audience and capture new opportunities.

7. Ad Copy and Landing Page Optimization:

Effective ad copy and landing page optimization play a critical role in driving conversions. Analyze ad performance, click-through rates, and bounce rates to identify areas for improvement. Craft compelling ad copy that aligns with campaign objectives and resonates with the target audience. Optimize landing pages to provide a seamless user experience, align with ad messaging, and have clear call-to-action (CTA) elements.

8. Continuous Monitoring and Performance Analysis:

Continuous monitoring and performance analysis are essential for campaign success. Regularly review campaign data, analyze key metrics, and identify trends or patterns. Utilize analytics platforms, such as Google Analytics, to gain insights into user behavior, traffic sources, and website engagement. Use these insights to refine targeting, optimize bidding, and improve overall campaign performance.

9. Competitor Analysis and Market Research:

Conducting competitor analysis and market research is crucial for staying competitive and identifying new opportunities. Analyze competitor strategies, identify industry trends, and assess market demands. Use this information to refine targeting, adjust bidding strategies, and differentiate ad campaigns to stand out in the market.

10. Continuous Optimization and Iteration:

PPC campaigns require ongoing optimization and iteration to stay relevant and effective. Continuously test and refine ad variations, landing pages, targeting options, and bidding strategies. Implement data-driven insights to make informed decisions and adjust campaigns based on performance metrics and market dynamics.

Conclusion:

PPC analytics and optimization are indispensable for maximizing the success of PPC campaigns. By utilizing analytics platforms, tracking key metrics, and implementing optimization techniques such as A/B testing, bid management, and keyword expansion, businesses can refine their campaigns, improve performance, and achieve their marketing goals. Conversion tracking and attribution modeling enable businesses to measure and optimize campaign effectiveness. Ad copy and landing page optimization drive higher engagement and conversion rates. Continuous monitoring, competitor analysis, and market research provide valuable insights for ongoing optimization. By leveraging the power of PPC analytics and implementing effective optimization strategies, businesses can make data-driven decisions, allocate budgets effectively, and drive maximum ROI from their PPC campaigns in the ever-evolving digital landscape.

5. Social Media Marketing

Social media marketing: Promote products, engage audiences, build brand awareness, and drive website traffic through compelling content, ads, and community interactions on social platforms.

5.1 Overview of Social Media Marketing

Social Media Marketing: Harnessing the Power of Online Engagement

Introduction:

Social media has revolutionized the way people connect, communicate, and consume content. As a result, social media platforms have become a valuable space for businesses to reach and engage with their target audience. Social media marketing leverages these platforms to build brand awareness, drive website traffic, foster customer relationships, and achieve marketing goals. In this article, we will provide an overview of social media marketing, exploring its benefits, key components, and best practices to help businesses harness the power of online engagement and maximize their success in the digital landscape.

1. Understanding Social Media Marketing:

Social media marketing involves the strategic use of social media platforms to promote products, services, and content. It encompasses a range of activities, including creating and sharing engaging content, running targeted ads, engaging with followers, and monitoring campaign performance. Social media marketing allows businesses to build brand identity, reach a wide audience, and foster meaningful connections with customers.

2. Benefits of Social Media Marketing:

Social media marketing offers numerous benefits for businesses. It provides an opportunity to increase brand visibility, as billions of people actively use social media platforms. Social media allows for precise targeting, ensuring that ads and content are shown to relevant audiences based on demographics, interests, and behaviors. Engagement on social media platforms helps businesses build brand loyalty and establish relationships with customers. Social media marketing also offers valuable insights and analytics, allowing businesses to measure campaign effectiveness, understand audience preferences, and make data-driven decisions.

3. Key Components of Social Media Marketing:

Social media marketing involves several key components. Developing a social media strategy is crucial, outlining campaign objectives, target audience, and key performance indicators (KPIs). Content creation plays a central role, requiring businesses to produce engaging and relevant posts, images, videos, and stories. Social media advertising enables businesses to reach wider audiences through targeted ads. Engagement and community management involve interacting with followers, responding to comments and messages, and fostering meaningful conversations. Monitoring and analytics allow businesses to measure campaign performance, track engagement, and gain insights into audience behavior.

4. Choosing the Right Social Media Platforms:

Choosing the right social media platforms is essential for reaching the target audience effectively. Facebook is the largest social media platform, offering diverse ad formats and extensive targeting options. Instagram is popular among younger audiences and is known for its visual content. Twitter allows for real-time engagement and is suitable for timely updates and customer interactions. LinkedIn caters to professionals and B2B audiences, making it ideal for industry networking and thought leadership. Pinterest focuses on visual discovery and is suitable for businesses in industries such as fashion, home decor, and food. Understanding the unique features and user demographics of each platform helps businesses select the most suitable ones for their marketing goals.

5. Content Strategy and Creation:

A robust content strategy is vital for successful social media marketing. It involves understanding the target audience, determining the appropriate tone and messaging, and planning a content calendar. Content should be engaging, informative, and relevant to the audience's interests. Visual content, including images and videos, often performs well on social media platforms. Live videos and stories provide opportunities for real-time engagement. Businesses should also consider user-generated content and influencer partnerships to enhance credibility and reach.

6. Social Media Advertising:

Social media advertising enables businesses to amplify their reach and target specific audience segments. Platforms like Facebook Ads, Instagram Ads, Twitter Ads, and LinkedIn Ads offer various ad formats, including image ads, video ads, carousel ads, and sponsored content. Advanced targeting options allow businesses to define their audience based on demographics, interests, behaviors, and more. Social media ads should be visually appealing, concise, and compelling to capture users' attention and drive engagement.

7. Engagement and Community Management:

Engagement and community management involve interacting with followers, responding to comments and messages, and fostering a sense of community. Engaging with followers helps build brand loyalty, enhance customer relationships, and encourage user-generated content. Consistency in posting and timely responses to queries and feedback are crucial for maintaining an active and engaged community. Social media monitoring tools can help streamline engagement efforts and track conversations around the brand.

8. Analytics and Performance Measurement:

Analytics and performance measurement provide valuable insights into the effectiveness of social media marketing efforts. Social media platforms offer built-in analytics dashboards that provide data on post reach, engagement and audience demographics. Additional analytics tools, such as Google Analytics, help track website traffic and conversions generated from social media platforms. Key metrics to track include follower growth, engagement rates, click-through rates (CTR), conversion rates, and return on ad spend (ROAS). Analyzing this data helps businesses understand campaign performance, identify trends, and make data-driven decisions to optimize their social media marketing efforts.

9. Influencer Marketing and Partnerships:

Influencer marketing involves collaborating with social media influencers to promote products or services. Influencers have established credibility and a loyal following, making them valuable advocates for businesses. Partnering with influencers allows businesses to tap into their audience and leverage their influence to drive brand awareness, engagement, and conversions. Careful selection of influencers based on relevance, audience alignment, and authenticity is essential for successful influencer marketing campaigns.

10. Continuous Adaptation and Optimization:

Social media marketing is an ever-evolving landscape, and businesses must continuously adapt their strategies and optimize their campaigns. Keeping up with platform updates, trends, and algorithm changes helps businesses stay relevant. Monitoring campaign performance, testing different ad formats, content types, and messaging, and analyzing audience behavior enable businesses to refine their strategies and achieve optimal results.

Conclusion:

Social media marketing offers businesses a powerful way to connect with their target audience, increase brand visibility, and achieve marketing goals. By understanding the key components of social media marketing, including content strategy, social media advertising, engagement, and analytics, businesses can build a strong online presence and foster meaningful customer relationships. Choosing the right social media platforms and developing compelling content are crucial for capturing audience attention. Monitoring campaign performance, analyzing data, and making data-driven decisions allow businesses to optimize their strategies and achieve maximum return on investment. By harnessing the power of social media marketing and adapting to the ever-changing digital landscape, businesses can thrive in the online world and drive meaningful business outcomes.

5.2 Social Media Platforms and Their Audiences

Social Media Platforms and Their Audiences: Reaching the Right Users for Effective Engagement

Introduction:

Social media platforms have become powerful channels for businesses to connect with their target audiences, build brand awareness, and drive engagement. However, each platform caters to a unique demographic and offers different features and functionalities. Understanding the characteristics and preferences of each platform's audience is crucial for businesses to tailor their social media marketing strategies effectively. In this article, we will explore the major social media platforms and their audiences, helping businesses identify the right platforms to reach their target users and achieve their marketing objectives.

1. Facebook: The All-in-One Social Network:

With over 2.8 billion monthly active users, Facebook is the largest social media platform. It appeals to a wide range of demographics, making it suitable for businesses targeting diverse audiences. Facebook's audience spans all age groups, with the majority falling in the 25-34 age range. It is especially popular among millennials and Generation X. Facebook offers a wide range of ad formats and targeting options, making it versatile for various marketing objectives.

2. Instagram: Visual Appeal and Millennial Dominance:

Instagram is a visually-oriented platform that emphasizes images and videos. It attracts a younger audience, with the majority falling between the ages of 18 and 34. Instagram's user base is particularly skewed towards millennials, making it an ideal platform for businesses targeting this demographic. It is highly effective for lifestyle brands, fashion, beauty, travel, and food industries. Instagram's ad formats, including Stories and shoppable posts, offer unique opportunities for engaging users.

3. Twitter: Real-Time Engagement and News:

Twitter is known for its real-time engagement and conversation-driven environment. It appeals to a broad range of users, including journalists, influencers, celebrities, and news enthusiasts. Twitter's audience tends to be more educated, with a higher income level. The platform is particularly suitable for businesses seeking timely engagement, customer service interactions, and sharing news and updates. Hashtags and trending topics enable businesses to participate in relevant conversations and increase brand visibility.

4. LinkedIn: The Professional Network:

LinkedIn is the leading social media platform for professionals and businesses. It caters to a primarily B2B audience and is popular among job seekers, recruiters, and industry professionals. LinkedIn's user base consists of professionals from various industries, making it an ideal platform for thought leadership, networking, and sharing industry-related content. LinkedIn Ads offers robust targeting options based on job titles, company size, and industry, allowing businesses to reach specific professional segments.

5. YouTube: Video Content and Entertainment:

YouTube is the largest video-sharing platform globally, attracting a broad range of users. It appeals to users of all ages and offers diverse content, including entertainment, educational videos, and tutorials. YouTube's audience tends to skew slightly younger, with a higher percentage of users falling between the ages of 18 and 34. It is an excellent platform for businesses that can leverage video content to engage with their audience effectively.

6. Pinterest: Visual Discovery and Inspiration:

Pinterest is a visual discovery platform that emphasizes user-generated content and allows users to curate collections of images and ideas. It appeals to a predominantly female audience, with interests ranging from fashion, home decor, DIY projects, recipes, and travel. Pinterest users actively seek inspiration and ideas, making it ideal for businesses in creative industries or those with visually appealing products. Pinterest's ad formats, including Promoted Pins, allow businesses to showcase products and drive traffic to their websites.

7. Snapchat: Millennial and Gen Z Engagement:

Snapchat is a multimedia messaging app popular among younger users, primarily millennials and Generation Z. It emphasizes ephemeral content, disappearing after a short period. Snapchat's audience is highly engaged and receptive to creative and interactive content. It offers various ad formats, including Snap Ads, Filters, and Lenses, allowing businesses to create immersive brand experiences.

8. TikTok: Short-Form Video and Viral Trends:

TikTok has quickly gained popularity, especially among Gen Z users. It is a platform for short-form videos, often featuring music and viral challenges. TikTok's audience is highly engaged, enthusiastic, and open to creative and entertaining content. The platform provides opportunities for businesses to leverage viral trends and engage with a younger demographic.

Conclusion:

Understanding the characteristics and preferences of each social media platform's audience is crucial for businesses to effectively reach their target users and achieve their marketing objectives. Facebook offers a broad reach and versatile ad formats, appealing to diverse demographics. Instagram's visual appeal and millennial dominance make it ideal for businesses in fashion, beauty, and lifestyle industries. Twitter's real-time engagement and news focus attract a diverse audience, particularly those seeking timely interactions. LinkedIn caters to professionals and B2B audiences, offering thought leadership and networking opportunities. YouTube's broad user base and video-centric environment are suitable for businesses leveraging video content. Pinterest's predominantly female audience seeks inspiration and ideas. Snapchat and TikTok engage younger audiences with interactive and viral content. By selecting the right social media platforms based on their audience demographics and preferences, businesses can effectively engage with their target users and achieve maximum results in their social media marketing efforts.

5.3 Creating Engaging Social Media Content

Crafting Engaging Social Media Content: Strategies for Captivating Your Audience

Introduction:

In the fast-paced world of social media, capturing and retaining the attention of your target audience is a constant challenge. Creating engaging social media content is essential for building brand awareness, driving user interaction, and ultimately achieving your marketing goals. In this article, we will explore effective strategies and best practices for crafting compelling and captivating social media content that resonates with your audience and encourages meaningful engagement.

1. Understand Your Target Audience:

Before creating social media content, it is crucial to have a deep understanding of your target audience. Research their demographics, interests, and preferences to tailor your content to their needs and desires. By understanding their motivations and pain points, you can create content that resonates and sparks interest.

2. Tell a Story:

Humans are wired to connect with stories. Incorporate storytelling into your social media content to evoke emotions and create a personal connection with your audience. Use narratives, anecdotes, or customer success stories to engage and captivate their attention.

3. Visual Appeal: Images and Videos:

Visual content has a higher impact and engagement rate on social media platforms. Incorporate eye-catching images, videos, infographics, and GIFs to capture attention and convey your message effectively. High-quality and aesthetically pleasing visuals will entice your audience to stop scrolling and engage with your content.

4. Embrace Authenticity:

Authenticity builds trust and fosters meaningful connections with your audience. Be transparent, genuine, and relatable in your social media content. Share behind-the-scenes glimpses, user-generated content, and real stories to establish an emotional bond with your audience.

5. Incorporate User-Generated Content:

User-generated content (UGC) not only reduces the burden of content creation but also increases engagement. Encourage your audience to create and share content related to your brand. Showcase UGC, such as customer reviews, testimonials, or user-submitted photos, to foster a sense of community and encourage participation.

6. Create Interactive Content:

Interactive content encourages active engagement from your audience. Polls, quizzes, contests, and interactive stories are effective tools to generate excitement and encourage participation. Ask questions, invite opinions, and prompt users to share their experiences to stimulate conversation.

7. Utilize Influencer Partnerships:

Collaborating with influencers in your industry can amplify your reach and credibility. Partner with relevant influencers to create sponsored content or to endorse your products/services. Their endorsement and influence can significantly impact your social media engagement and attract a wider audience.

8. Embrace Humor and Emotion:

Humor and emotion are powerful drivers of engagement. Inject humor into your content when appropriate and use emotional triggers to evoke empathy or excitement. Memes, puns, and clever captions can help create a positive and memorable experience for your audience.

9. Craft Compelling Headlines and Captions:

Craft attention-grabbing headlines and captions that pique curiosity and encourage click-throughs. Use persuasive language, ask thought-provoking questions, or provide valuable insights to entice your audience to engage with your content further.

10. Optimize Posting Schedule and Frequency:

Timing and consistency play a vital role in social media engagement. Understand your audience's behavior and preferences to determine the best times to post content. Additionally, maintain a consistent posting schedule to stay on your audience's radar without overwhelming them.

11. Encourage Social Sharing and Tagging:

Encourage your audience to share your content and tag their friends or colleagues. Run contests or giveaways that require users to tag others, increasing your content's reach and visibility. By leveraging social sharing, you can tap into your audience's networks and attract new followers.

12. Monitor and Respond to Engagement:

Engagement is a two-way street. Monitor comments, messages, and mentions to promptly respond and engage with your audience. Show appreciation for positive feedback, address concerns, and foster conversations to build a loyal community.

13. Analyze and Iterate:

Regularly analyze the performance of your social media content. Track engagement metrics, such as likes, shares, comments, and click-through rates. Utilize analytics tools to gain insights into your audience's preferences and adjust your content strategy accordingly.

Conclusion:

Crafting engaging social media content requires a deep understanding of your target audience, creativity, and strategic planning. By incorporating storytelling, visual appeal, authenticity, and interactive elements, you can captivate your audience's attention and foster meaningful engagement. Leverage user-generated content, influencer partnerships, and humor to amplify your reach and drive social sharing. Optimize your posting schedule, monitor engagement, and respond promptly to build a loyal community. Regularly analyze performance metrics to gain insights into your audience's preferences and refine your content strategy. By employing these strategies and best practices, you can create compelling social media content that resonates with your audience, enhances your brand presence, and ultimately drives the desired results in the dynamic world of social media.

5.4 Social Media Advertising

Unleashing the Power of Social Media Advertising: Driving Success with Targeted Campaigns

Introduction:

Social media advertising has transformed the digital marketing landscape, providing businesses with powerful tools to reach and engage their target audience. With billions of active users across various platforms, social media advertising offers unparalleled reach and targeting capabilities. In this article, we will explore the benefits of social media advertising, discuss key platforms and ad formats, and delve into effective strategies for driving success with targeted campaigns.

1. The Benefits of Social Media Advertising:

Social media advertising offers numerous benefits for businesses. It allows precise audience targeting based on demographics, interests, behaviors, and more, ensuring that ads reach the most relevant users. Social media platforms provide extensive reach, with billions of active users, enabling businesses to increase brand visibility and expand their customer base. The interactive nature of social media platforms facilitates engagement, encourages user interaction, and drives conversions. Social media advertising also offers robust analytics and tracking capabilities, allowing businesses to measure campaign performance, optimize strategies, and achieve a higher return on investment (ROI).

2. Key Social Media Advertising Platforms:

Major social media platforms provide diverse advertising opportunities. Facebook Ads offers a vast user base and comprehensive targeting options, making it suitable for businesses of all sizes and industries. Instagram Ads leverage the platform's visual appeal and engagement to reach a predominantly millennial audience. Twitter Ads enable real-time engagement and conversation-driven campaigns, ideal for timely promotions and news updates. LinkedIn Ads target professionals and B2B audiences, providing thought leadership and networking opportunities. YouTube Ads tap into the world's largest video-sharing platform, allowing businesses to leverage video content to engage users. Each platform offers unique features and caters to specific audience segments, enabling businesses to tailor their strategies accordingly.

3. Social Media Advertising Formats:

Social media platforms provide various advertising formats to suit different campaign goals and audience preferences. Image ads are visually engaging and can be used across platforms to convey brand messaging. Video ads allow businesses to tell compelling stories and showcase products or services. Carousel ads enable multiple images or videos within a single ad unit, providing more information and interaction. Collection ads on Facebook and Instagram display a collection of products that users can explore. Lead generation ads help businesses capture user information directly within the platform. Sponsored content integrates seamlessly within users' feeds, blending in with organic content while promoting brand messages. Each ad format offers unique advantages, and businesses should consider their objectives and audience preferences when selecting the most suitable formats.

4. Defining Campaign Objectives:

To run successful social media advertising campaigns, businesses must establish clear objectives. Whether the goal is to drive brand awareness, increase website traffic, generate leads, or boost sales, defining campaign objectives helps determine the right targeting strategies, ad formats, and budget allocation. Clearly defined objectives provide a framework for measuring success and optimizing campaigns for maximum impact.

5. Targeting and Audience Segmentation:

One of the strengths of social media advertising is its advanced targeting capabilities. Businesses can define target audiences based on demographics, interests, behaviors, and more. Audience segmentation allows businesses to create tailored messages for specific user segments. Custom audience targeting enables businesses to reach existing customers or retarget website visitors. Lookalike audience targeting helps expand reach by finding users similar to existing customers. By leveraging precise targeting and audience segmentation, businesses can ensure that their ads are seen by the most relevant users, increasing the chances of engagement and conversion.

6. Ad Copy and Creative Elements:

Compelling ad copy and creative elements are crucial for capturing users' attention and driving engagement. Ad copy should be concise, compelling, and aligned with campaign objectives. Use persuasive language, compelling calls-to-action, and a clear value proposition. Creative elements, such as high-quality images, captivating videos, or interactive content, should be visually appealing and reflect the brand's identity. A/B testing can help determine the most effective ad variations and optimize creative elements for maximum impact.

7. Budget Allocation and Bid Management:

Effectively allocating budgets and managing bids are vital for optimizing social media advertising campaigns. Businesses should set realistic budgets based on campaign objectives and consider testing different strategies to find the optimal allocation. Continuous monitoring of campaign performance, including metrics like click-through rates, conversion rates, and cost per acquisition, allows businesses to adjust bids and optimize campaigns for better results. Automated bidding strategies and bid adjustments based on performance data can streamline bid management and maximize ROI.

8. Ad Performance Tracking and Optimization:

Tracking ad performance is crucial for optimizing social media advertising campaigns. Social media platforms provide analytics dashboards that offer insights into impressions, clicks, conversions, and audience engagement. Leveraging these analytics, businesses can identify top-performing ads, ad placements, and targeting strategies. Continuous optimization involves making data-driven decisions to improve campaign performance. Businesses should monitor key metrics, test different strategies, refine targeting, and adjust ad copy or creative elements to enhance engagement and achieve better results.

9. Remarketing and Retargeting:

Remarketing and retargeting are effective techniques for re-engaging users who have previously interacted with a business. By targeting users who have visited the website, engaged with ads, or interacted with social media profiles, businesses can deliver personalized messages and increase the chances of conversion

Remarketing campaigns can be tailored based on user behavior and specific actions taken. Retargeting campaigns can leverage dynamic ads that show users the products or services they previously viewed, reminding them to complete their purchase.

10. Testing and Experimentation:

Continuous testing and experimentation are essential for optimizing social media advertising campaigns. A/B testing allows businesses to compare different variations of ads, targeting strategies, or ad formats to determine which ones yield better results. Testing can include variations in ad copy, images, calls-to-action, or targeting parameters. Experimentation helps businesses discover new opportunities, stay ahead of the competition, and continuously improve campaign performance.

Conclusion:

Social media advertising offers businesses unparalleled reach, precise targeting capabilities, and robust analytics for optimizing campaign performance. By defining clear campaign objectives, leveraging the strengths of different social media platforms and ad formats, and tailoring content to the target audience, businesses can create effective and engaging social media advertising campaigns. Through strategic budget allocation, bid management, and continuous optimization, businesses can maximize ROI and drive desired outcomes. Social media advertising provides businesses with the opportunity to reach their target audience, build brand awareness, drive engagement, and ultimately achieve their marketing goals in the ever-evolving digital landscape.

5.5 Social Media Analytics and Reporting

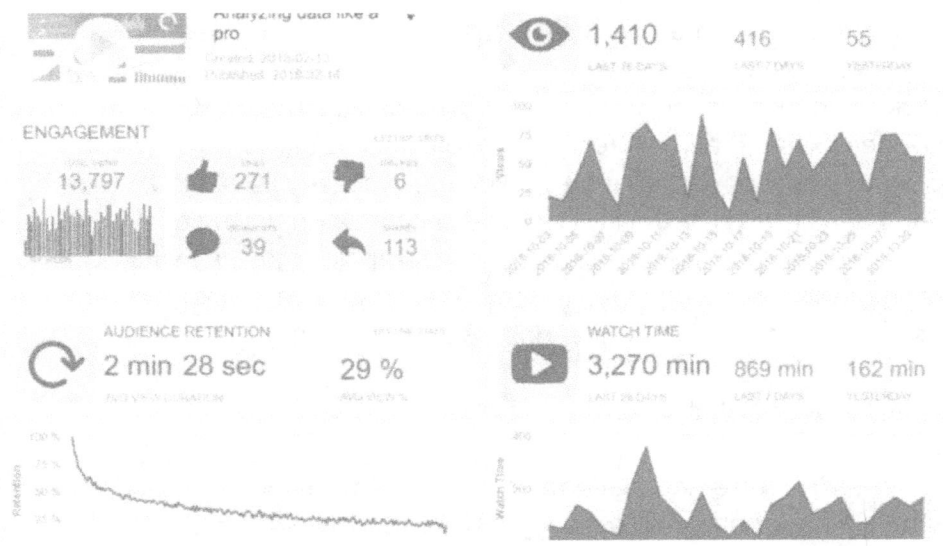

Harnessing the Power of Social Media Analytics and Reporting: Unlocking Insights for Strategic Success

Introduction:

Social media platforms have become invaluable channels for businesses to connect with their audience, build brand awareness, and drive engagement. To optimize social media marketing efforts, it is crucial to track and analyze the performance of campaigns. Social media analytics and reporting provide valuable insights into audience behavior, content effectiveness, and campaign success. In this article, we will explore the importance of social media analytics, discuss key metrics to track, delve into analytics tools and platforms, and highlight best practices for reporting to drive strategic decision-making and maximize results.

1. The Importance of Social Media Analytics:

Social media analytics offer valuable insights into the effectiveness of marketing efforts. By tracking and analyzing key metrics, businesses can gain a deeper understanding of their audience, measure campaign performance, identify trends, and make data-driven decisions. Social media analytics enable businesses to optimize content strategies, refine targeting, allocate resources effectively, and achieve maximum return on investment (ROI).

2. Key Metrics to Track in Social Media Analytics:

There are several key metrics businesses should track to assess social media performance. Engagement metrics, such as likes, comments, shares, and click-through rates, indicate audience interaction and content effectiveness. Reach and impressions help evaluate brand visibility and campaign reach. Conversion metrics, such as website clicks, lead generation, and purchases, measure the impact of social media on driving desired actions. Follower growth and audience demographics provide insights into audience growth and composition. Social media sentiment analysis can assess the sentiment of conversations around the brand.

3. Social Media Analytics Tools and Platforms:

Various analytics tools and platforms can help businesses track and measure social media performance. Most social media platforms, such as Facebook Insights, Twitter Analytics, and LinkedIn Analytics, provide built-in analytics dashboards with detailed metrics and insights. Third-party analytics tools like Hootsuite, Sprout Social, and Buffer offer comprehensive analytics and reporting capabilities across multiple social media platforms. Google Analytics can be integrated with social media platforms to track website traffic and conversions driven by social media referrals. These tools provide data on audience demographics, engagement, reach, conversion, and more, empowering businesses to monitor and optimize their social media marketing efforts.

4. Best Practices for Social Media Reporting:

Effective social media reporting is essential for extracting insights and communicating performance to stakeholders. To create impactful reports, businesses should:

a. Define Objectives: Clearly articulate the goals and objectives of the social media campaigns to provide context for the reported data.

b. Select Relevant Metrics: Focus on metrics that align with the campaign objectives and provide actionable insights.

c. Visualize Data: Present data in a visually appealing and easily understandable format, using charts, graphs, and infographics to convey key findings.

d. Provide Context: Interpret the data and provide context around the performance, highlighting trends, successes, and areas for improvement.

e. Benchmark Against Goals: Compare actual performance to predefined goals or industry benchmarks to gauge success and identify areas for optimization.

f. Customize for Stakeholders: Tailor the reporting format and level of detail to the needs of different stakeholders, such as executives, marketing teams, or clients.

g. Continuously Improve: Gather feedback on the reporting process and iterate to enhance the relevance and effectiveness of future reports.

5. Leveraging Social Media Insights for Strategic Decision-Making:

Social media analytics provide actionable insights that can inform strategic decision-making. Analyzing audience demographics helps refine targeting strategies and develop content that resonates with specific segments. Engagement metrics guide content optimization, allowing businesses to understand what types of posts or campaigns generate the most interaction. Conversion metrics help identify the most effective channels and campaigns for driving website traffic, lead generation, or sales. Sentiment analysis provides insights into audience perception and sentiment towards the brand. By leveraging social media insights, businesses can refine their content strategies, optimize ad campaigns, allocate resources effectively, and drive strategic decision-making across various aspects of their marketing efforts.

Conclusion:

Social media analytics and reporting are essential for optimizing social media marketing efforts. By tracking and analyzing key metrics, businesses can gain valuable insights into audience behavior, content effectiveness, and campaign success. Social media analytics tools and platforms offer comprehensive data and reporting capabilities, enabling businesses to monitor and optimize their social media performance. By following best practices for reporting, businesses can effectively communicate results and insights to stakeholders. Leveraging social media insights empowers businesses to make data-driven decisions, refine targeting strategies, optimize content, and allocate resources effectively. With the power of social media analytics and reporting, businesses can unlock valuable insights, drive strategic decision-making, and maximize the impact of their social media marketing efforts in today's dynamic digital landscape.

6. Email Marketing

Email marketing: Utilizing email campaigns to connect with customers, deliver targeted messages, nurture leads, promote products, and drive conversions for business growth and customer engagement.

6.1 Introduction to Email Marketing

The Power of Email Marketing: Unlocking Success Through Targeted Communication

Introduction:

Email marketing has long been a cornerstone of digital marketing strategies, and for good reason. It provides businesses with a direct line of communication to engage with their audience, build relationships, and drive conversions. In an era of evolving digital channels, email marketing remains a powerful tool for delivering personalized and targeted messages to the right people at the right time. In this article, we will explore the benefits of email marketing, discuss key components of an effective email marketing strategy, and highlight best practices for success.

1. The Benefits of Email Marketing:

Email marketing offers several advantages for businesses. It allows for direct and personalized communication, enabling businesses to tailor messages to individual recipients based on their preferences, behaviors, and demographics. Email marketing is cost-effective, providing a high return on investment (ROI) compared to other marketing channels. It is also highly scalable, allowing businesses to reach a large audience with minimal effort. Email marketing provides measurable results, with metrics like open rates, click-through rates, and conversions, enabling businesses to track the success of their campaigns. Furthermore, email marketing helps foster customer relationships, build brand loyalty, and drive repeat business.

2. Key Components of an Effective Email Marketing Strategy:

To create a successful email marketing strategy, businesses should consider the following components:

a. Goal Definition: Clearly define the objectives of your email marketing campaigns, whether it's driving sales, increasing brand awareness, or nurturing leads.

b. Audience Segmentation: Segment your email list based on factors like demographics, purchase history, engagement levels, or interests to deliver targeted and relevant content.

c. Permission-Based Marketing: Obtain consent from recipients to receive emails, ensuring compliance with data protection regulations and maintaining a healthy and engaged subscriber base.

d. Compelling Content: Craft compelling and relevant content that captures the recipients' attention, adds value, and encourages action. Personalize emails based on the recipient's preferences, past interactions, or purchase history.

e. Engaging Subject Lines: Create attention-grabbing subject lines that entice recipients to open the email. A well-crafted subject line can significantly impact open rates.

f. Responsive Design: Optimize emails for various devices and screen sizes, ensuring a seamless experience for recipients, regardless of the device they use.

g. Call-to-Action (CTA): Include clear and compelling CTAs to guide recipients towards the desired action, whether it's making a purchase, signing up for a webinar, or downloading a resource.

h. Testing and Optimization: Continuously test different elements of your emails, such as subject lines, content, visuals, and CTAs, to identify what resonates best with your audience and optimize future campaigns.

3. Types of Email Campaigns:

There are various types of email campaigns that businesses can leverage based on their objectives and target audience:

a. Welcome Emails: Sent to new subscribers to introduce your brand, set expectations, and provide valuable information or incentives.

b. Newsletter Emails: Regularly scheduled emails that provide updates, industry news, helpful tips, and content relevant to your audience's interests.

c. Promotional Emails: Designed to drive sales, these emails highlight special offers, discounts, or new product releases to encourage recipients to make a purchase.

d. Abandoned Cart Emails: Sent to users who have added items to their cart but left without completing the purchase, reminding them to return and complete the transaction.

e. Event or Webinar Emails: Used to promote upcoming events, conferences, webinars, or workshops, providing information and encouraging registrations.

f. Customer Retention Emails: Aimed at retaining existing customers, these emails may include exclusive offers, loyalty rewards, or personalized recommendations.

4. Email Marketing Best Practices:

To maximize the impact of your email marketing campaigns, consider the following best practices:

a. Build a Quality Email List: Focus on growing a quality subscriber base by using opt-in forms, providing incentives, and ensuring you have permission to send emails.

b. Personalization and Segmentation: Customize emails based on recipient preferences, demographics, or past interactions to deliver relevant content and increase engagement.

c. Test and Optimize: Continuously test different elements of your emails, such as subject lines, CTAs, or content, to identify what resonates best with your audience and refine your strategy accordingly.

d. Monitor and Analyze Metrics: Track key metrics such as open rates, click-through rates, conversions, and unsubscribe rates to measure the success of your campaigns and make data-driven decisions.

e. Optimize for Mobile: Ensure your emails are mobile-friendly and responsive to cater to the growing number of users accessing emails on mobile devices.

f. Compliance and Privacy: Adhere to data protection regulations, honor unsubscribes promptly, and maintain transparency in your email practices.

Conclusion:

Email marketing remains a powerful tool for businesses to engage with their audience, build relationships, and drive conversions. By creating personalized and targeted messages, businesses can deliver value to their subscribers, nurture leads, and foster brand loyalty. With careful planning and execution, an effective email marketing strategy can drive measurable results, increase sales, and contribute to long-term business success. By following best practices, continuously testing and optimizing campaigns, and monitoring key metrics, businesses can leverage the power of email marketing to connect with their audience, deliver valuable content, and achieve their marketing objectives in the ever-evolving digital landscape.

6.2 Building An Email List And Segmentation

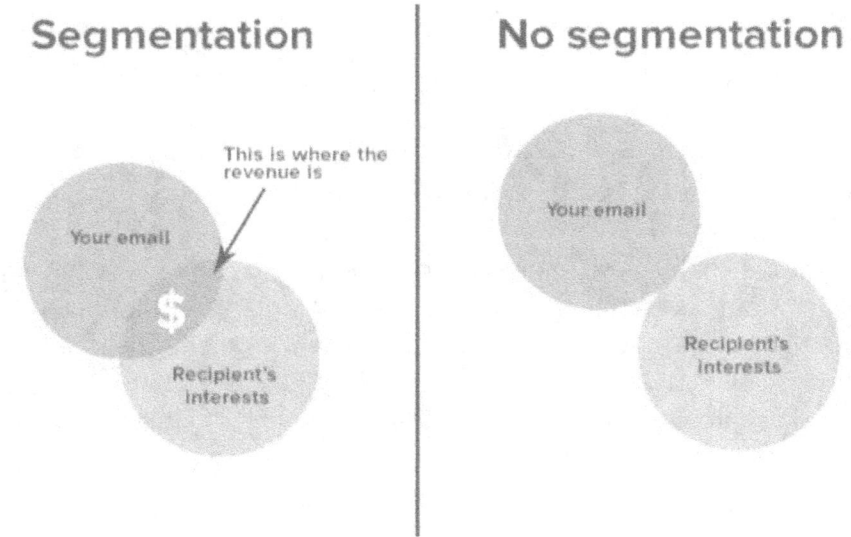

Building an Email List and Segmentation: Maximizing Engagement and Conversion

Introduction:

Building an email list and effectively segmenting it is a critical step in creating successful email marketing campaigns. A well-curated email list allows businesses to connect with their target audience, nurture relationships, and drive conversions. In this article, we will explore strategies for building an email list, discuss the importance of segmentation, and highlight best practices to maximize engagement and conversion rates.

1. Strategies for Building an Email List:

Building an email list requires a strategic approach. Consider the following strategies to grow your subscriber base:

a. Opt-In Forms and Lead Magnets: Place opt-in forms on your website, landing pages, and blog posts, offering valuable incentives such as ebooks, whitepapers, discounts, or exclusive content to encourage sign-ups.

b. Content Upgrades: Create content upgrades, such as bonus resources or checklists, relevant to your blog posts or articles. Offer them in exchange for visitors' email addresses.

c. Social Media Engagement: Utilize social media platforms to engage with your audience and promote sign-ups. Direct followers to your opt-in forms or lead magnet landing pages.

d. Webinars and Events: Host webinars or events and require registration, capturing participants' email addresses in the process.

e. Partnerships and Collaborations: Collaborate with complementary businesses or influencers in your industry to cross-promote and expand your reach.

f. Offline Opportunities: Collect email addresses at trade shows, conferences, or in-store events by offering raffles, giveaways, or sign-up sheets.

2. Importance of Email List Segmentation:

Email list segmentation involves dividing your subscribers into specific groups based on shared characteristics, allowing you to deliver targeted and personalized content. Segmentation is crucial for maximizing engagement and conversion rates:

a. Personalization: Segmented emails allow you to deliver content that is relevant to specific subscriber interests, preferences, or behaviors, increasing the likelihood of engagement and conversion.

b. Increased Open and Click-Through Rates: Segmented emails often yield higher open rates and click-through rates as recipients perceive the content as more relevant and valuable.

c. Improved Email Deliverability: Targeted emails reduce the likelihood of spam complaints and unsubscribes, leading to better email deliverability rates.

d. Nurturing Customer Relationships: Segmentation enables businesses to tailor their communication and build stronger relationships with subscribers by addressing their specific needs and pain points.

e. Precise Campaign Evaluation: Segmentation allows for accurate analysis of campaign performance within different segments, enabling businesses to make data-driven decisions and optimize future campaigns.

3. Key Segmentation Factors:

When segmenting your email list, consider the following key factors:

a. Demographics: Divide subscribers based on demographics such as age, gender, location, or occupation. This can help tailor content specific to their characteristics and preferences.

b. Behavior and Engagement: Segment subscribers based on their interactions with your emails, such as open rates, click-through rates, or purchase history. This allows for targeted campaigns to re-engage inactive subscribers or reward highly engaged ones.

c. Purchase History: Divide subscribers based on their purchase behavior, enabling personalized recommendations, cross-selling, or upselling opportunities.

d. Interests and Preferences: Segment subscribers according to their stated interests, preferences, or subscription preferences. This enables businesses to deliver content that matches their specific areas of interest.

e. Customer Journey Stage: Segment subscribers based on where they are in the customer journey, such as leads, first-time buyers, or loyal customers. This allows for tailored nurturing and conversion-focused campaigns.

4. Best Practices for Email List Segmentation:

To effectively segment your email list, consider the following best practices:

a. Collect Relevant Data: Gather the necessary information at the point of sign-up or through progressive profiling over time to ensure accurate segmentation.

b. Automate Segmentation: Utilize email marketing automation tools to automatically segment subscribers based on their behaviors, interactions, or preferences.

c. Start with Broad Segments: Begin with broader segmentation categories and gradually refine them as you gather more data and insights.

d. Test and Refine: Continuously test and refine your segments, evaluating their performance and adjusting as needed to improve engagement and conversion rates.

e. Maintain Clean and Updated Data: Regularly clean your email list, removing inactive or invalid addresses, and updating subscriber information to ensure segmentation accuracy.

f. Personalize Content: Tailor your email content to each segment's interests, preferences, or behaviors, providing valuable and personalized messaging that resonates with your subscribers.

Conclusion:

Building an email list and segmenting it effectively are integral to successful email marketing campaigns. By employing strategies to grow your subscriber base and capturing relevant data, businesses can engage with their target audience and nurture customer relationships. Implementing segmentation based on demographics, behavior, interests, and customer journey stage allows for targeted and personalized campaigns, leading to higher engagement and conversion rates. By following best practices, continuously refining segments, and delivering content that resonates with each group, businesses can maximize the impact of their email marketing efforts and achieve long-term success in connecting with their audience and driving desired outcomes.

6.3 Designing Effective Email Campaigns

Designing Effective Email Campaigns: Strategies for Engaging and Converting Subscribers

Introduction:

Email campaigns are a powerful tool in the digital marketer's arsenal, allowing businesses to communicate directly with their audience, nurture relationships, and drive conversions. However, designing effective email campaigns requires careful planning and execution. In this article, we will explore strategies for designing email campaigns that captivate subscribers, deliver value, and achieve desired outcomes.

1. Define Campaign Objectives:

Before designing an email campaign, clearly define its objectives. Whether it's promoting a product, driving website traffic, nurturing leads, or boosting sales, having a clear objective helps shape the content, structure, and call-to-action (CTA) of the campaign.

2. Craft Attention-Grabbing Subject Lines:

Subject lines play a crucial role in getting subscribers to open your emails. Craft subject lines that are concise, compelling, and personalized. Use persuasive language, create a sense of urgency, or pose intriguing questions to entice recipients to open your emails.

3. Create Engaging and Relevant Content:

The content of your email should be engaging, valuable, and relevant to your subscribers. Personalize the content based on their preferences, demographics, or previous interactions. Use a conversational tone, incorporate storytelling, and provide information that solves their problems or meets their needs.

4. Visual Appeal and Responsive Design:

Incorporate visually appealing elements into your emails to grab attention and enhance engagement. Use high-quality images, compelling graphics, or videos to convey your message effectively. Ensure that your emails are optimized for different devices and screen sizes, utilizing responsive design to provide a seamless experience for subscribers.

5. Clear Call-to-Action (CTA):

Include a clear and compelling CTA in your emails to guide subscribers towards the desired action. Make the CTA stand out with contrasting colors or buttons, use action-oriented language, and clearly communicate the benefit of taking that action. Whether it's making a purchase, signing up for an event, or downloading a resource, the CTA should be prominent and easy to follow.

6. Test and Optimize:

Testing is crucial for designing effective email campaigns. A/B test different elements such as subject lines, email content, CTA placement, or visuals to identify what resonates best with your audience. Continuously optimize your campaigns based on the insights gained from testing, refining your approach to achieve better engagement and conversion rates.

7. Personalization and Segmentation:

Personalization and segmentation are key to designing effective email campaigns. Tailor your emails to specific segments based on demographics, interests, behavior, or previous interactions. Deliver personalized content that resonates with each segment, increasing engagement and conversion rates.

8. Automation and Drip Campaigns:

Leverage email marketing automation to design drip campaigns that deliver a series of targeted emails based on specific triggers or actions. Set up automated workflows that nurture leads, onboard new customers, or re-engage inactive subscribers. Automation helps deliver timely and relevant content while saving time and effort.

9. Testimonials, Social Proof, and User-generated Content:

Incorporate social proof elements such as testimonials, reviews, or user-generated content into your email campaigns. Showcase positive experiences and feedback from satisfied customers to build trust and credibility, encouraging subscribers to take action.

10. Monitor and Analyze Metrics:

Monitor and analyze key email metrics such as open rates, click-through rates, conversions, and unsubscribe rates to evaluate the success of your campaigns. Use analytics tools to gain insights into subscriber behavior, identify trends, and refine your strategies based on data-driven decisions.

11. Consistency and Frequency:

Maintain consistency in your email campaigns by establishing a regular sending schedule. However, be mindful of frequency to avoid overwhelming subscribers. Finding the right balance between staying in touch and avoiding email fatigue is crucial for maintaining engagement.

12. Compliance and Best Practices:

Adhere to email marketing best practices and ensure compliance with data protection regulations. Obtain consent from subscribers, provide clear unsubscribe options, and honor opt-out requests promptly. Follow email deliverability best practices, avoid spam triggers, and maintain a clean and updated email list.

Conclusion:

Designing effective email campaigns requires a thoughtful and strategic approach. By defining clear objectives, crafting attention-grabbing subject lines, creating engaging and relevant content, and incorporating visually appealing elements, businesses can captivate subscribers and drive desired actions. Personalization, segmentation, and automation help deliver targeted and timely emails that resonate with individual segments. Testing and optimization allow for continuous improvement and better results over time. By monitoring key metrics, analyzing data, and following best practices, businesses can design email campaigns that engage subscribers, build relationships, and ultimately convert them into loyal customers, contributing to the success of their overall marketing efforts.

6.4 Email Automation and Personalization

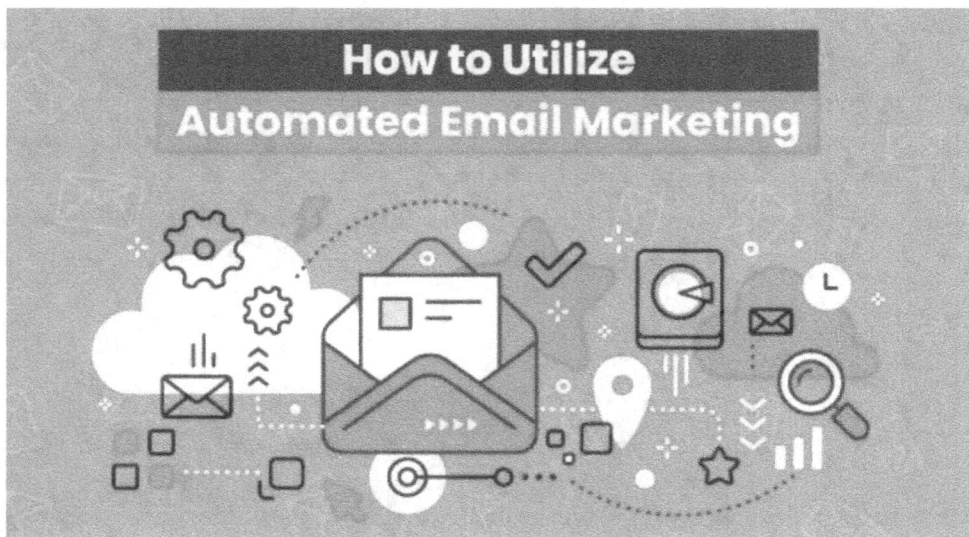

Unleashing the Power of Email Automation and Personalization: Enhancing Engagement and Driving Conversions

Introduction:

Email marketing has evolved from simple one-time campaigns to sophisticated automation and personalization strategies. Leveraging email automation and personalization allows businesses to deliver targeted, timely, and relevant content to their subscribers. In this article, we will explore the benefits of email automation and personalization, discuss key strategies and techniques, and highlight best practices for maximizing engagement and driving conversions.

1. The Benefits of Email Automation:

Email automation streamlines marketing efforts, saving time and resources while delivering personalized messages. Key benefits include:

a. Timely and Relevant Communication: Automation enables businesses to send emails triggered by specific actions or events, ensuring subscribers receive timely and relevant content.

b. Nurturing Customer Relationships: Automated drip campaigns nurture leads, onboard new customers, and re-engage inactive subscribers, building stronger customer relationships.

c. Efficiency and Scalability: Automation allows businesses to deliver consistent messaging to a large subscriber base, without manually managing individual emails.

d. Consistency and Branding: Automated emails maintain a consistent brand voice and style, reinforcing brand identity and recognition.

e. Data-Driven Decision Making: Automation provides insights into subscriber behavior, allowing businesses to optimize campaigns based on data-driven decisions.

2. Implementing Email Automation:

To implement email automation effectively, consider the following strategies:

a. Define Customer Journeys: Map out the different stages of the customer journey and identify key touchpoints where automated emails can be triggered.

b. Segmentation and Personalization: Segment your email list based on demographics, behavior, or preferences, and tailor automated emails to each segment.

c. Set Triggers and Workflow: Set triggers based on subscriber actions or events, such as welcome emails, abandoned cart reminders, or birthday offers. Develop workflows that guide subscribers through their unique journeys.

d. Content Strategy: Create compelling and relevant content that aligns with the subscriber's stage in the customer journey, addressing their specific needs and pain points.

e. Test and Optimize: Continuously test and refine your automated campaigns, analyzing metrics like open rates, click-through rates, and conversions. Optimize your workflows and content to improve engagement and drive desired outcomes.

3. The Power of Email Personalization:

Personalization is a key driver of email marketing success. By tailoring emails to individual subscribers, businesses can create a personalized experience that increases engagement and conversion rates. Benefits include:

a. Higher Open and Click-through Rates: Personalized emails grab attention and resonate with recipients, leading to higher open rates and click-through rates.

b. Improved Customer Experience: Personalization makes subscribers feel valued, understood, and more likely to engage with the content.

c. Enhanced Relevance and Conversion: Personalized emails deliver content that aligns with subscribers' interests, preferences, or past interactions, increasing the likelihood of conversion.

d. Relationship Building: Personalization helps foster stronger relationships with subscribers by providing customized recommendations, exclusive offers, or relevant content.

4. Strategies for Email Personalization:

To incorporate effective email personalization into your campaigns, consider the following strategies:

a. Personalized Subject Lines: Use the subscriber's name or other personalized elements in subject lines to grab attention and increase open rates.

b. Dynamic Content: Utilize dynamic content blocks within emails to display personalized product recommendations, location-specific offers, or customized messaging.

c. Behavioral Triggers: Use subscriber behavior, such as past purchases, website interactions, or email engagement, to trigger personalized emails that align with their actions.

d. Lifecycle Emails: Craft personalized emails for specific stages of the customer journey, providing relevant content and offers based on where subscribers are in the funnel.

e. Personalized Recommendations: Leverage subscriber data to provide personalized product recommendations, similar to what they have shown interest in or purchased previously.

5. Best Practices for Email Automation and Personalization:

To make the most of email automation and personalization, follow these best practices:

a. Data Collection and Management: Collect and maintain accurate subscriber data to fuel your automation and personalization efforts. Ensure compliance with data protection regulations.

b. Integration with CRM and Analytics: Integrate your email marketing platform with customer relationship management (CRM) systems and analytics tools to gather comprehensive data and insights.

c. Test and Monitor: Continuously test and monitor the performance of your automated campaigns and personalized content. Analyze metrics and iterate to optimize results.

d. Don't Overdo It: Maintain a balance between automation and personalization, ensuring that emails feel genuine and not overly automated.

e. Permission and Unsubscribe Options: Provide clear opt-in and opt-out options, and honor unsubscribe requests promptly to maintain a healthy and engaged subscriber base.

Conclusion:

Email automation and personalization have revolutionized the way businesses engage with their audience. Leveraging automation enables timely and relevant communication, while personalization creates tailored experiences that drive engagement and conversions. By implementing email automation, businesses can streamline their marketing efforts, nurture customer relationships, and achieve scalability. Pairing automation with personalization helps businesses deliver individualized content that resonates with subscribers, increasing open rates, click-through rates, and overall campaign success. By following best practices, continuously testing and optimizing, and utilizing subscriber data effectively, businesses can unlock the power of email automation and personalization, enhancing engagement, and driving desired outcomes in their email marketing efforts.

6.5 Email Marketing Analytics

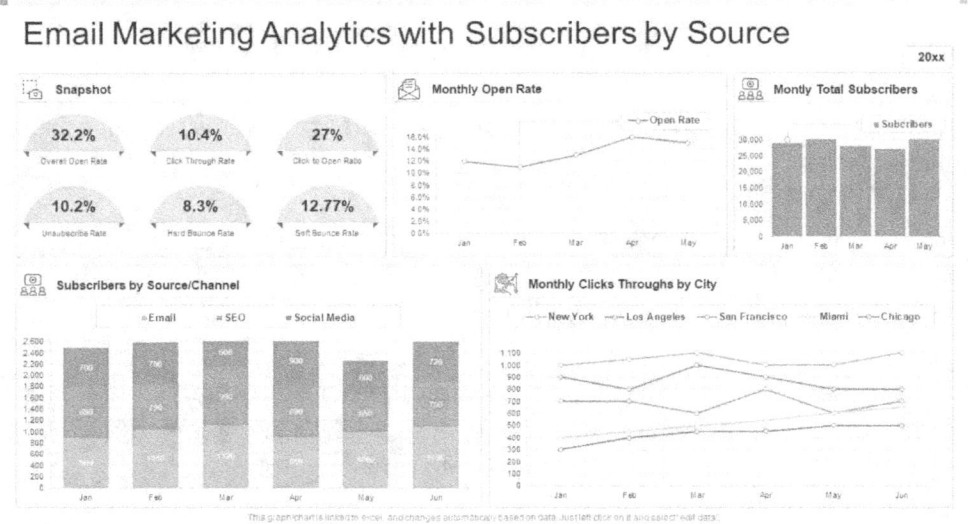

Unleashing the Power of Email Marketing Analytics: Driving Insights for Success

Introduction:

In the ever-evolving landscape of digital marketing, email marketing continues to be a powerful tool for businesses to engage with their audience, nurture relationships, and drive conversions. However, to truly maximize the impact of email campaigns, it is crucial to harness the power of email marketing analytics. In this article, we will explore the importance of email marketing analytics, discuss key metrics to track, delve into analytics tools and platforms, and highlight best practices for utilizing data-driven insights to achieve email marketing success.

1. The Importance of Email Marketing Analytics:

Email marketing analytics provides businesses with valuable insights into the performance of their email campaigns. By tracking and analyzing key metrics, businesses can gain a deeper understanding of subscriber behavior, campaign effectiveness, and overall email marketing success. Email marketing analytics offers benefits such as:

- Measurement of Success: Analytics enables businesses to measure the success of their email campaigns based on key performance indicators (KPIs), such as open rates, click-through rates, conversion rates, and revenue generated.

- Data-Driven Decision Making: Analytics provides data and insights that can guide strategic decision-making, allowing businesses to optimize their email campaigns, refine targeting, and tailor content to achieve desired outcomes.

- Continuous Improvement: By analyzing metrics and identifying areas for improvement, businesses can iterate and optimize their email marketing strategies to enhance engagement, conversion, and overall campaign success.

2. Key Metrics to Track in Email Marketing Analytics:

To evaluate the effectiveness of email campaigns, businesses should track and analyze key metrics. Some essential metrics include:

- Open Rate: The percentage of recipients who opened the email. It indicates the effectiveness of subject lines, sender reputation, and subscriber engagement.

- Click-Through Rate (CTR): The percentage of recipients who clicked on a link within the email. It measures the engagement and interest generated by the content and call-to-action (CTA).

- Conversion Rate: The percentage of recipients who completed the desired action, such as making a purchase, signing up for a webinar, or downloading a resource. It reflects the effectiveness of the email in driving conversions.

- Bounce Rate: The percentage of emails that were not delivered due to invalid email addresses or other delivery issues. It helps assess the quality and cleanliness of the email list.

- Unsubscribe Rate: The percentage of subscribers who opted out of receiving future emails. It indicates subscriber dissatisfaction or lack of interest in the content.

3. Email Marketing Analytics Tools and Platforms:

There are several email marketing analytics tools and platforms that provide comprehensive data and insights for evaluating campaign performance. Some popular options include:

- Email Service Provider (ESP) Analytics: Most ESPs offer built-in analytics dashboards that provide metrics on open rates, click-through rates, unsubscribes, and more.

- Google Analytics: By integrating Google Analytics with email campaigns, businesses can track website traffic, conversions, and user behavior driven by email referrals.

- Third-Party Analytics Tools: There are specialized analytics tools designed specifically for email marketing, such as Mailchimp, Campaign Monitor, and Sendinblue. These tools offer robust analytics capabilities, advanced segmentation options, and A/B testing features.

4. Best Practices for Email Marketing Analytics:

To effectively leverage email marketing analytics, consider the following best practices:

- Set Clear Objectives: Define clear goals and objectives for your email campaigns to align your analytics efforts and measure success against predefined benchmarks.

- Segment Your Data: Analyze metrics based on different segments, such as demographics, engagement levels, or purchase history, to gain deeper insights into subscriber behavior and preferences.

- Regularly Monitor Metrics: Continuously track and monitor key email marketing metrics to identify trends, patterns, and areas for improvement. Regular analysis helps in optimizing campaigns for better performance.

- A/B Testing: Conduct A/B tests to compare different elements of your emails, such as subject lines, CTAs, or content, to identify what resonates best with your audience and refine your strategies.

- Combine Qualitative and Quantitative Analysis: While quantitative metrics provide numerical data, consider qualitative factors such as subscriber feedback, survey responses, or customer testimonials to gain a comprehensive understanding of the impact of your email campaigns.

- Continuously Optimize: Use data-driven insights from analytics to make informed decisions and continuously optimize your email marketing strategies for better engagement, conversion, and ROI.

Conclusion:

Email marketing analytics plays a vital role in driving success and maximizing the impact of email campaigns. By tracking and analyzing key metrics, businesses can gain valuable insights into subscriber behavior, campaign effectiveness, and overall performance. Email marketing analytics provides a data-driven foundation for optimizing campaigns, refining targeting, and tailoring content to achieve desired outcomes. By utilizing analytics tools and platforms, businesses can access comprehensive data, segment their audience, and measure the success of their email marketing efforts. Following best practices, such as setting clear objectives, regularly monitoring metrics, and combining qualitative and quantitative analysis, empowers businesses to make data-driven decisions and continuously optimize their email marketing strategies. By harnessing the power of email marketing analytics, businesses can enhance engagement, drive conversions, and achieve greater success in their email marketing endeavors.

7. Content Marketing

Content marketing: Creating valuable, relevant content to attract, engage, and retain a target audience, driving profitable customer action and building brand authority.

7.1 What is Content Marketing?

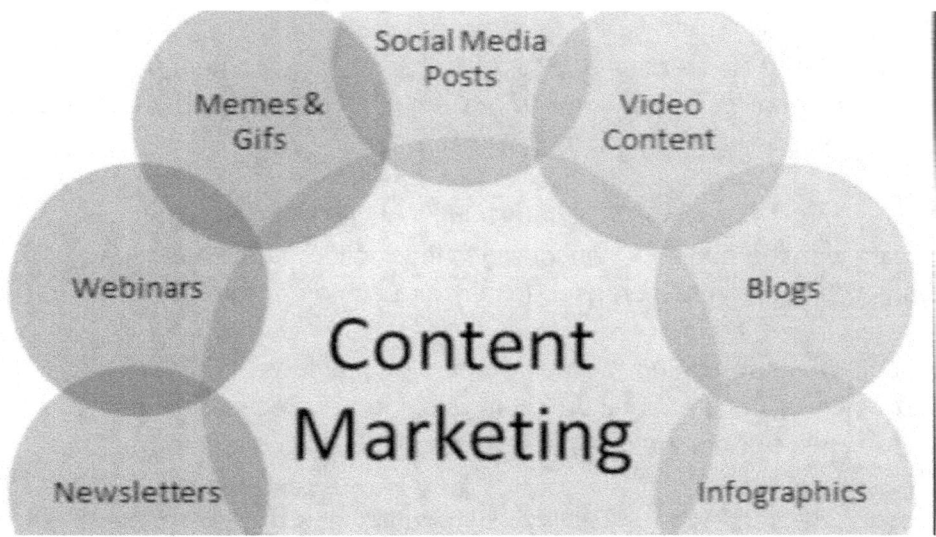

Content Marketing: A Strategic Approach to Engaging and Nurturing Audiences

Introduction:

In today's digital landscape, where consumers are inundated with advertisements and promotional messages, businesses need to find innovative ways to connect with their target audience. Content marketing has emerged as a powerful strategy to engage, educate, and build long-term relationships with customers. In this article, we will explore the concept of content marketing, its significance in modern marketing, key components of a successful content marketing strategy, and best practices for creating compelling and impactful content.

1. Defining Content Marketing:

Content marketing is a strategic approach that involves creating and distributing valuable, relevant, and consistent content to attract and retain a clearly defined audience. Unlike traditional advertising, content marketing aims to provide value to the audience by offering information, entertainment, or insights, rather than overtly promoting products or services. The goal is to build trust, establish credibility, and position the brand as a thought leader in the industry.

2. The Significance of Content Marketing:

Content marketing offers several benefits to businesses:

a. Building Brand Awareness and Visibility: Compelling content helps businesses establish a strong online presence, increase brand visibility, and reach a wider audience.

b. Driving Engagement and Building Relationships: Valuable content resonates with the audience, encourages interaction, and fosters long-term relationships, leading to increased loyalty and customer retention.

c. Educating and Informing: Content marketing provides an opportunity to educate the audience about industry trends, best practices, and solutions to their problems, positioning the brand as a trusted source of information.

d. Boosting Search Engine Visibility: High-quality and relevant content improves search engine rankings, driving organic traffic to the website and increasing brand visibility.

e. Supporting Sales and Conversion: Well-crafted content helps to nurture leads, guide customers through the buyer's journey, and influence purchasing decisions.

3. Key Components of a Successful Content Marketing Strategy:

To develop a successful content marketing strategy, businesses should consider the following components:

a. Audience Research: Understand the target audience's demographics, needs, pain points, and preferences to create content that resonates with them.

b. Clear Goals and Objectives: Define specific goals for your content marketing efforts, such as increasing brand awareness, driving website traffic, or generating leads.

c. Content Creation and Curation: Develop a content plan that includes a mix of original content creation, curated content from trusted sources, and user-generated content.

d. Content Distribution Channels: Identify the appropriate channels to reach the target audience, such as social media platforms, blogs, email newsletters, or video-sharing platforms.

e. Consistency and Frequency: Maintain a consistent publishing schedule to keep the audience engaged and establish brand credibility.

f. SEO and Keyword Optimization: Optimize content for search engines by incorporating relevant keywords, meta tags, and optimizing titles and descriptions.

g. Performance Measurement and Analysis: Track key metrics, such as website traffic, engagement rates, conversion rates, and social media shares, to evaluate the success of your content marketing efforts.

4. Creating Compelling and Impactful Content:

To create content that resonates with the audience and drives engagement, consider the following best practices:

a. Audience-Centric Approach: Tailor content to address the needs, interests, and pain points of the target audience, delivering value and solving their problems.

b. Storytelling: Use storytelling techniques to captivate the audience, evoke emotions, and create a memorable brand experience.

c. Visual Appeal: Incorporate visually appealing elements, such as images, infographics, or videos, to enhance the visual impact and make the content more shareable.

d. Originality and Uniqueness: Offer unique perspectives, insights, or experiences that differentiate your content from competitors and provide a fresh perspective.

e. Call-to-Action (CTA): Include clear and compelling CTAs to guide the audience towards the desired action, such as signing up for a newsletter, downloading a resource, or making a purchase.

f. Continuous Learning and Adaptation: Stay updated with industry trends, audience preferences, and content performance metrics. Continuously refine your content strategy based on insights and feedback.

5. Repurposing and Amplifying Content:

Maximize the impact of your content by repurposing it across different formats and channels. Convert blog posts into videos, infographics, or podcasts. Share content on social media platforms, guest post on industry websites, or collaborate with influencers to reach new audiences.

Conclusion:

Content marketing has become an integral part of modern marketing strategies, providing businesses with a powerful approach to engage, educate, and build relationships with their audience. By creating valuable and relevant content, businesses can establish themselves as industry thought leaders, drive brand awareness, and nurture customer loyalty. A successful content marketing strategy involves understanding the target audience, setting clear objectives, creating compelling content, and utilizing the right distribution channels. By incorporating storytelling, visual appeal, and strong calls-to-action, businesses can create content that resonates with the audience and drives desired outcomes. Continuous monitoring, analysis, and adaptation are essential for refining the content strategy and maximizing its impact. Embrace the power of content marketing to connect with your audience, deliver value, and achieve long-term marketing success.

7.2 Content Strategy and Planning

Mastering Content Strategy and Planning: A Roadmap for Effective Marketing

Introduction:

Content strategy and planning are crucial components of successful marketing efforts. A well-defined content strategy guides businesses in creating and delivering valuable, relevant, and consistent content that resonates with their target audience. In this article, we will explore the importance of content strategy and planning, discuss key steps to develop an effective content strategy, delve into the process of content planning, and highlight best practices for achieving content marketing success.

1. The Importance of Content Strategy:

Content strategy provides a strategic framework for businesses to align their content efforts with their overall marketing objectives. It helps businesses:

- Define Goals and Objectives: Content strategy ensures that content creation and distribution are aligned with specific business goals, such as increasing brand awareness, driving website traffic, or generating leads.

- Audience Understanding: A content strategy involves deep audience research and understanding to identify their needs, preferences, and pain points. This enables businesses to create content that resonates with the target audience.

- Consistency and Brand Voice: A content strategy establishes guidelines for maintaining consistency in brand messaging, tone, and style across all content channels. This consistency builds brand recognition and trust.

- Optimization for Search Engines: Content strategy incorporates search engine optimization (SEO) techniques, ensuring that content is discoverable by search engines and attracts organic traffic.

- Efficient Resource Allocation: Content strategy helps allocate resources effectively by identifying content types, channels, and distribution strategies that provide the best return on investment.

2. Developing an Effective Content Strategy:

To develop a robust content strategy, consider the following steps:

- Define Objectives: Clearly articulate the goals and objectives you want to achieve through your content marketing efforts.

- Identify Target Audience: Conduct thorough audience research to understand their demographics, needs, preferences, and behaviors. This knowledge will shape the content strategy.

- Determine Key Messages: Identify the key messages you want to convey through your content to align with your brand values, positioning, and unique selling propositions.

- Select Content Formats: Determine the most appropriate content formats (e.g., blog posts, videos, infographics) that resonate with your target audience and effectively communicate your messages.

- Develop a Content Calendar: Create a content calendar that outlines the topics, publication dates, and distribution channels for each piece of content.

- Incorporate SEO Strategies: Integrate SEO techniques, such as keyword research and optimization, into your content strategy to enhance search engine visibility.

- Establish Measurement Metrics: Define metrics to track and measure the success of your content strategy, such as engagement rates, conversions, or brand sentiment.

3. The Process of Content Planning:

Effective content planning ensures the systematic creation and distribution of content aligned with the content strategy. Follow these steps for efficient content planning:

- Content Ideation: Brainstorm and research content ideas that align with your objectives, target audience, and industry trends.

- Content Creation: Develop high-quality, relevant, and engaging content that addresses the needs and interests of your audience.

- Content Optimization: Optimize your content for SEO by incorporating relevant keywords, meta tags, and other SEO best practices.

- Content Publishing: Determine the most suitable channels and platforms to distribute your content, such as your website, blog, social media, or email newsletters.

- Content Promotion: Develop a promotional strategy to amplify the reach of your content, leveraging social media, influencer collaborations, paid advertising, or guest posting.

- Content Monitoring and Analysis: Continuously track the performance of your content, analyze key metrics, and gather insights to refine your content planning and strategy.

4. Best Practices for Content Strategy and Planning:

To achieve content marketing success, adhere to these best practices:

- Audience-Centric Approach: Prioritize the needs, preferences, and pain points of your target audience in your content strategy and planning.

- Consistency and Branding: Maintain consistency in brand messaging, tone, and visual identity across all content channels to reinforce brand recognition and trust.

- Value and Relevance: Create content that delivers value to your audience, addresses their challenges, and offers solutions or insights.

- Collaboration and Team Alignment: Involve stakeholders from different departments to ensure collaboration and alignment in content planning and execution.

- Content Repurposing: Leverage existing content by repurposing it into different formats or adapting it for different channels to maximize its reach and impact.

- Continuous Evaluation and Optimization: Regularly monitor and analyze content performance metrics, and use data-driven insights to optimize your content strategy and planning.

Conclusion:

A well-defined content strategy and effective content planning are critical elements of successful marketing campaigns. A robust content strategy aligns content creation and distribution with business objectives, target audience needs, and brand positioning. It establishes consistency, optimizes for search engines, and ensures resource allocation efficiency. Content planning, on the other hand, involves ideation, creation, optimization, distribution, promotion, and analysis of content. Following best practices, such as an audience-centric approach, consistency in branding, value-driven content creation, collaboration, repurposing, and continuous optimization, leads to content marketing success. By developing a strong content strategy, implementing efficient content planning processes, and continuously refining your approach based on analytics insights, you can engage your audience, build brand credibility, and achieve your marketing goals.

7.3 Creating Compelling Content

Crafting Compelling Content: Strategies for Captivating and Engaging Your Audience

Introduction:

In the digital age, where attention spans are fleeting and competition for online visibility is fierce, creating compelling content has become essentia for businesses to connect with their target audience. Compelling content grabs attention, resonates with readers, and drives them to take desired actions. In this article, we will explore the art of crafting compelling content, discussing key strategies, techniques, and best practices that will help you captivate and engage your audience effectively.

1. Understanding Your Target Audience:

The foundation of compelling content creation lies in understanding your target audience. Conduct thorough research to identify their demographics, needs, preferences, and pain points. This knowledge will enable you to tailor your content to address their specific interests and challenges.

2. Emphasizing Value and Relevance:

Compelling content provides value to the audience by delivering insights, solutions, or entertainment. Focus on creating content that is informative, educational, inspiring, or entertaining. It should be relevant to your audience's interests and align with their goals.

3. Telling Stories:

Storytelling is a powerful technique to engage readers emotionally and create a memorable impact. Craft narratives that connect with your audience's experiences, evoke emotions, and convey your message effectively. Use storytelling elements such as characters, conflict, and resolution to make your content more engaging and relatable.

4. Incorporating Visual Elements:

Visual elements such as images, infographics, videos, and interactive media enhance the visual appeal of your content. They capture attention, break up text, and convey information in a more engaging and digestible format. Use high-quality visuals that are relevant to your content and align with your brand identity.

5. Writing with Clarity and Simplicity:

Compelling content is easy to read and understand. Use clear and concise language, avoiding jargon or complex terminology. Break down information into bite-sized chunks, use headings and subheadings, and incorporate bullet points or numbered lists to improve readability.

6. Evoking Emotions:

Emotional appeal is a powerful way to create a connection with your audience. Craft content that evokes emotions such as joy, surprise, empathy, or inspiration. Use storytelling, relatable anecdotes, or powerful imagery to trigger emotional responses and deepen the engagement with your content.

7. Engaging Headlines and Introductions:

Compelling headlines and introductions are crucial for grabbing attention and enticing readers to continue reading. Craft attention-grabbing headlines that convey the value or benefit of your content. In introductions, hook readers with compelling storytelling, thought-provoking questions, or intriguing statements.

8. Incorporating Data and Research:

Back up your content with credible data, statistics, and research findings. This adds credibility, authority, and enhances the value of your content. Use reputable sources and cite references to strengthen the trustworthiness of your information.

9. Encouraging Interaction and Conversation:

Compelling content sparks conversation and engagement. Encourage readers to share their thoughts, opinions, or experiences in the comments section or through social media. Respond to comments and engage in dialogue to foster a sense of community and connection.

10. Using Calls-to-Action (CTAs):

Include clear and compelling calls-to-action (CTAs) within your content to guide readers towards the desired action. Whether it's signing up for a newsletter, downloading a resource, or making a purchase, the CTA should be prominent and clearly communicate the benefit of taking that action.

11. Iterating and Refining:

Creating compelling content is an iterative process. Continuously monitor the performance of your content, gather feedback from your audience, and analyze metrics such as engagement rates, social shares, and conversions. Use these insights to refine your content strategy and improve future content creation.

Conclusion:

Crafting compelling content requires a strategic and thoughtful approach. By understanding your target audience, emphasizing value and relevance, incorporating storytelling, visuals, and emotions, and using engaging headlines and introductions, you can capture the attention and engage your audience effectively. Encourage interaction, utilize CTAs, and continuously iterate and refine your content based on analytics insights. Compelling content has the power to inspire, educate, entertain, and build meaningful connections with your audience. By consistently creating compelling content, you can establish your brand as a trusted source, increase brand loyalty, and drive desired actions. Embrace these strategies and techniques to create content that captivates, engages, and leaves a lasting impact on your audience.

7.4 Content Distribution And Promotion

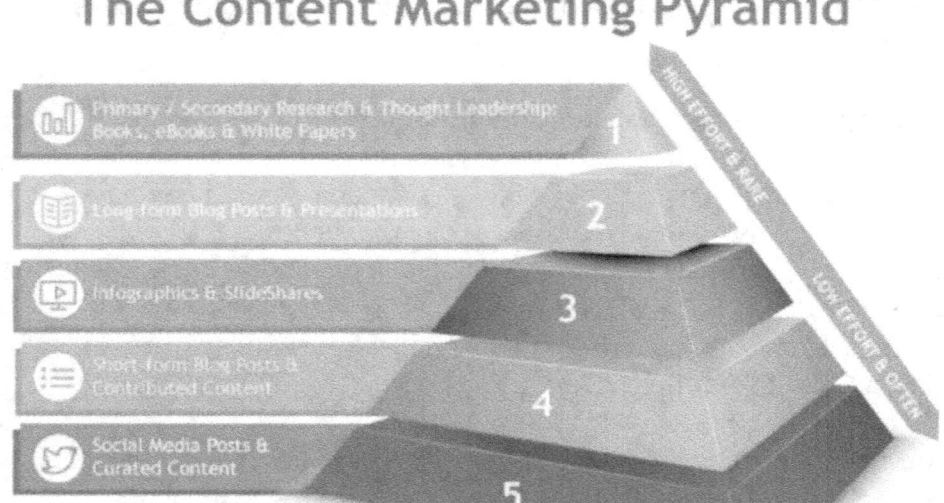

Mastering Content Distribution and Promotion: Strategies for Amplifying Your Reach and Impact

Introduction:

Creating high-quality content is just the first step in a successful content marketing strategy. To truly maximize its impact, you need to ensure that your content reaches the right audience. Content distribution and promotion play a critical role in amplifying your reach, driving traffic to your content, and increasing engagement. In this article, we will explore effective strategies for content distribution and promotion, covering key channels, techniques, and best practices that will help you expand your audience and enhance the visibility of your content.

1. Understanding Content Distribution:

Content distribution involves disseminating your content across various channels and platforms to reach a wider audience. It ensures that your content is available and accessible to your target audience where they spend their time online.

2. Choosing the Right Distribution Channels:

Identify the most suitable distribution channels for your content based on your target audience's preferences and behavior. These channels can include your website, blog, social media platforms, email newsletters, content syndication platforms, influencer collaborations, guest posting, or industry publications.

3. Tailoring Content for Different Channels:

Adapt your content to fit the requirements and nuances of each distribution channel. Optimize content length, format, and messaging to ensure it resonates with the specific platform and its audience. For example, create shorter, visually appealing snippets for social media or repurpose long-form content into slideshows or infographics.

4. Leveraging Social Media:

Social media platforms offer immense opportunities for content distribution and promotion. Identify the platforms where your audience is most active, share your content consistently, engage with your audience, and leverage features such as hashtags, mentions, and social sharing buttons to expand your reach.

5. Email Marketing and Newsletters:

Utilize email marketing and newsletters to distribute your content directly to your subscribers. Craft compelling email subject lines, personalize the content based on subscriber preferences, and include prominent CTAs to encourage readers to engage with your content.

6. Content Syndication and Collaboration:

Consider syndicating your content on reputable platforms or collaborating with industry influencers and publications to expand your reach. This allows you to tap into their existing audience and gain exposure to new readers who may not have discovered your content otherwise.

7. Search Engine Optimization (SEO):

Optimize your content for search engines to increase its visibility in organic search results. Conduct keyword research, optimize titles, meta descriptions, headers, and alt tags, and ensure your content provides valuable information that aligns with search intent.

8. Paid Advertising:

Supplement your organic distribution efforts with paid advertising to accelerate your content's visibility. Utilize platforms like Google Ads, social media advertising, or native advertising to target specific demographics or interests and drive traffic to your content.

9. Influencer Outreach and Partnerships:

Collaborate with influencers or thought leaders in your industry who have a strong following and influence over your target audience. By leveraging their authority and reach, you can expand the visibility of your content and attract new readers.

10. Analytics and Optimization:

Monitor and analyze the performance of your content distribution channels using analytics tools. Track metrics such as website traffic, engagement rates, click-through rates, and conversions. Use these insights to optimize your distribution strategies, identify successful channels, and refine your approach for maximum impact.

11. Consistency and Iteration:

Maintain a consistent content distribution schedule to keep your audience engaged and build brand recognition. Continuously evaluate the performance of your distribution efforts, experiment with different channels and techniques, and iterate based on the data and feedback you receive.

Conclusion:

Content distribution and promotion are vital components of a successful content marketing strategy. By choosing the right distribution channels, tailoring content for different platforms, leveraging social media, email marketing, and influencers, optimizing for search engines, and utilizing paid advertising, you can amplify your reach and attract a wider audience. Regularly monitor and analyze the performance of your distribution efforts, adapt your strategies based on data-driven insights, and iterate for continuous improvement. Remember, effective content distribution and promotion go hand in hand with creating high-quality content. By combining compelling content with strategic distribution, you can increase engagement, drive traffic, and achieve your content marketing goals. Embrace these strategies and best practices to ensure your content reaches its intended audience and makes a lasting impact.

7.5 Content Marketing Metrics And Measurement

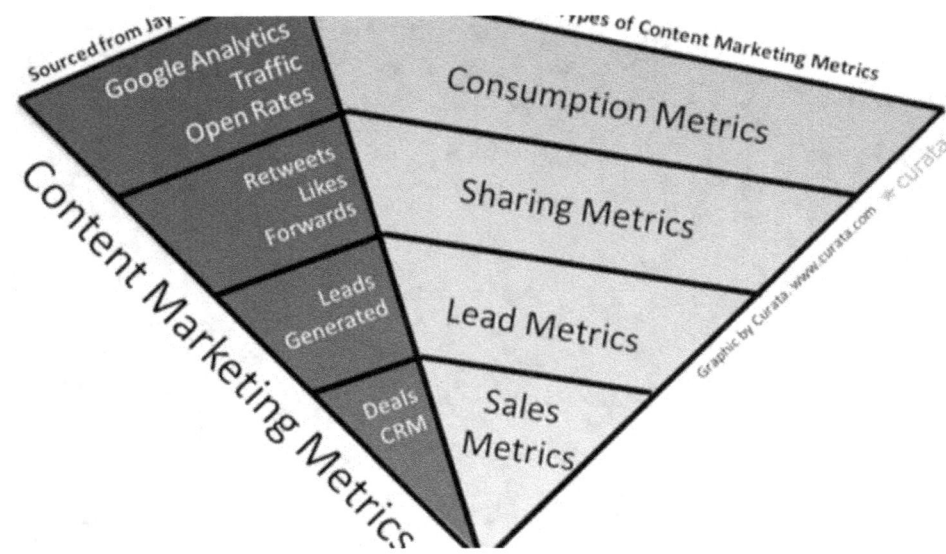

Decoding Content Marketing Metrics and Measurement: Tracking Success for Data-Driven Insights

Introduction:

Content marketing is a powerful strategy for businesses to engage their audience and drive desired outcomes. To evaluate the effectiveness of content marketing efforts, it is crucial to measure and analyze key metrics. Content marketing metrics provide valuable insights into audience engagement, content performance, and overall marketing success. In this article, we will explore the importance of content marketing metrics and measurement, discuss key metrics to track, delve into analytics tools and platforms, and highlight best practices for utilizing data-driven insights to optimize content marketing strategies.

1. The Importance of Content Marketing Metrics:

Content marketing metrics provide tangible evidence of the impact and effectiveness of content efforts. By measuring key metrics, businesses can:

- Evaluate Audience Engagement: Metrics such as page views, time on page, bounce rates, and social shares help gauge the level of audience engagement with the content.

- Assess Content Performance: Metrics like click-through rates, conversion rates, and lead generation metrics provide insights into how well the content is performing in driving desired actions.

- Refine Content Strategy: Metrics enable businesses to identify what types of content resonate with the audience, which channels drive the most traffic, and where improvements can be made.

- Prove ROI: Metrics help measure the return on investment (ROI) of content marketing efforts by tracking metrics tied to revenue, customer acquisition, or cost savings.

2. Key Metrics to Track in Content Marketing:

To evaluate the success of content marketing efforts, businesses should track and analyze the following key metrics:

- Consumption Metrics: Page views, unique visitors, time on page, bounce rates, and scroll depth provide insights into how users consume content and their level of engagement.

- Engagement Metrics: Social shares, comments, likes, and click-through rates measure the level of audience interaction and the effectiveness of content in driving engagement.

- Conversion Metrics: Conversion rates, lead generation metrics, email sign-ups, and form submissions help assess the content's ability to convert visitors into customers or leads.

- SEO Metrics: Organic search traffic, keyword rankings, backlinks, and search engine visibility reflect the content's performance in search engine results pages (SERPs).

- Revenue Metrics: Metrics tied to revenue, such as sales attributed to content, customer lifetime value, or average revenue per user, provide insights into the direct impact of content on revenue generation.

3. Analytics Tools and Platforms:

There are several analytics tools and platforms that can help businesses track and measure content marketing metrics. Some popular options include:

- Google Analytics: A widely used tool for tracking website traffic, audience behavior, and conversion metrics.

- Social Media Analytics: Platforms like Facebook Insights, Twitter Analytics, and LinkedIn Analytics provide valuable data on audience engagement, reach, and content performance within those specific channels.

- Email Marketing Analytics: Email marketing platforms offer metrics such as open rates, click-through rates, and conversions tied to email campaigns.

- Content Management Systems (CMS): Many CMS platforms have built-in analytics capabilities, providing insights into content performance directly within the platform.

4. Best Practices for Content Marketing Measurement:

To effectively measure content marketing success, consider the following best practices:

- Define Clear Objectives: Establish specific goals and objectives that align with your overall content marketing strategy.

- Identify Relevant Metrics: Choose metrics that directly relate to your objectives and provide meaningful insights into the effectiveness of your content.

- Set Benchmarks: Establish benchmarks based on historical data or industry standards to measure progress and compare performance.

- Regular Monitoring and Reporting: Continuously monitor and analyze metrics, and create regular reports to track progress and communicate results.

- A/B Testing: Conduct A/B tests to compare different versions of content and determine what resonates best with your audience.

- Integrated Data Analysis: Integrate data from various sources to gain a holistic view of content marketing performance and identify correlations or trends.

- Continuous Improvement: Use insights gained from metrics to refine content strategy, optimize performance, and adapt to evolving audience needs.

Conclusion:

Content marketing metrics and measurement are essential for tracking the effectiveness and impact of content efforts. By measuring key metrics related to audience engagement, content performance, conversions, SEO, and revenue, businesses can gain valuable insights into the success of their content marketing strategies. Utilizing analytics tools and platforms provides the necessary data to evaluate performance and make data-driven decisions. By following best practices such as setting clear objectives, choosing relevant metrics, regular monitoring and reporting, A/B testing, and continuous improvement, businesses can optimize their content marketing strategies and drive better results. Embrace the power of content marketing metrics to track success, make informed decisions, and continually refine your content strategy for maximum impact and ROI.

8. Influencer Marketing

Influencer marketing: Partnering with social media personalities to promote products, leveraging their influence to reach a wider audience and drive brand exposure and sales.

8.1 Introduction To Influencer Marketing

Introduction to Influencer Marketing: Leveraging the Power of Influence for Successful Brand Collaborations

Introduction:

In today's digitally connected world, influencer marketing has emerged as a dynamic and impactful strategy for brands to connect with their target audience. By collaborating with influential individuals who possess a dedicated following, brands can leverage the power of influence to enhance brand visibility, credibility, and engagement. In this article, we will explore the concept of influencer marketing, its growing significance in the digital landscape, the benefits it offers to brands, and key considerations for implementing successful influencer marketing campaigns.

1. Understanding Influencer Marketing:

Influencer marketing involves partnering with individuals who have established credibility, expertise, or a substantial following within a specific niche or industry. These influencers have the ability to sway the opinions, behaviors, and purchasing decisions of their audience through their authenticity and expertise. By leveraging their influence, brands can reach a wider audience, create meaningful connections, and drive desired actions.

2. The Significance of Influencer Marketing:

Influencer marketing has gained significant momentum due to several factors:

- Consumer Trust and Engagement: Influencers have cultivated a loyal and engaged audience, resulting in a higher level of trust and credibility among their followers. Collaborating with influencers allows brands to tap into this trust and connect with their target consumers in an authentic and relatable manner.

- Social Media Dominance: The rise of social media platforms has provided influencers with a powerful platform to share their expertise, stories, and recommendations. Brands can leverage the reach and engagement of influencers on these platforms to amplify their brand messages and connect with their desired audience effectively.

- Ad Blockers and Ad Fatigue: Traditional advertising methods often face challenges such as ad blockers and audience fatigue. Influencer marketing offers an alternative approach that bypasses these obstacles by integrating brand messages seamlessly into the influencers' content.

3. Benefits of Influencer Marketing:

Influencer marketing provides numerous benefits for brands:

- Increased Brand Awareness: Partnering with influencers exposes brands to a broader audience, extending their reach and boosting brand visibility.

- Authenticity and Trust: Influencers are seen as authentic voices within their niche, and their recommendations carry weight among their followers. By collaborating with influencers, brands can tap into this authenticity and establish trust with their target audience.

- Targeted Audience Reach: Influencers often have a specific demographic or niche audience, allowing brands to connect with a more targeted consumer base that aligns with their ideal customer profile.

- Content Creation and Engagement: Influencers are skilled content creators who can develop engaging and impactful content. Through collaborations, brands can tap into this expertise to create compelling and shareable content that resonates with their audience.

- Influencer Insights: Collaborating with influencers provides brands with valuable insights into consumer behavior, preferences, and trends within their target market.

4. Implementing Successful Influencer Marketing Campaigns:

To execute effective influencer marketing campaigns, brands should consider the following steps:

- Define Objectives and Target Audience: Clearly outline campaign objectives and identify the specific audience segments you want to reach through influencer collaborations.

- Research and Identify Influencers: Conduct thorough research to identify influencers who align with your brand values, have an engaged audience, and cater to your target demographics.

- Authentic Relationship Building: Foster genuine relationships with influencers by engaging with their content, understanding their audience, and offering value before approaching them for collaborations.

- Clear Communication and Expectations: Clearly communicate campaign goals, guidelines, and expectations to influencers to ensure brand alignment and mutual understanding.

- Creative Collaboration: Involve influencers in the creative process to leverage their expertise and ensure content resonates with their audience while aligning with brand messaging.

- Tracking and Measurement: Establish key performance indicators (KPIs) and track relevant metrics such as reach, engagement, conversions, and sentiment to evaluate campaign effectiveness.

- Compliance and Transparency: Ensure compliance with advertising regulations and disclose sponsored content transparently to maintain trust and transparency with the audience.

Conclusion:

Influencer marketing has revolutionized the way brands connect with consumers in the digital age. By partnering with influential individuals, brands can tap into the power of influence to enhance brand visibility, credibility, and engagement. The significance of influencer marketing lies in its ability to authentically connect with target audiences, leveraging the trust and credibility that influencers have cultivated. Through collaborations with influencers, brands can amplify their reach, build brand loyalty, and drive desired actions. By understanding the fundamentals of influencer marketing, harnessing the benefits it offers, and implementing strategic and authentic influencer collaborations, brands can unlock the potential for successful brand partnerships and meaningful connections in the ever-evolving digital landscape. Embrace influencer marketing as a valuable strategy to build brand awareness, connect with your target audience, and achieve marketing success.

8.2 Identifying And Engaging With Influencers

Unlocking the Power of Influencers: Strategies for Identifying and Engaging with Key Influencers

Introduction:

Influencer marketing has become a vital strategy for brands to reach their target audience and establish authentic connections. However, the success of an influencer marketing campaign hinges on identifying the right influencers and effectively engaging with them. In this article, we will explore key strategies for identifying influencers, discuss methods for evaluating their suitability for collaborations, and highlight best practices for engaging with influencers to build meaningful and mutually beneficial relationships.

1. Defining Your Influencer Criteria:

Before embarking on an influencer search, it is crucial to define your influencer criteria. Consider factors such as audience demographics, niche relevance, engagement levels, and alignment with your brand values and messaging. Clearly outlining your criteria will help streamline the identification process.

2. Conducting Thorough Research:

Thorough research is essential to identify influencers who align with your brand and target audience. Utilize social media platforms, influencer databases, and industry-specific websites to search for influencers in your niche. Examine their content, engagement rates, follower demographics, and the authenticity of their audience.

3. Evaluating Influencer Reach and Engagement:

While follower count is important, it's equally crucial to assess an influencer's engagement levels. Look for influencers with a dedicated and engaged audience, as this indicates their ability to drive conversations and influence their followers.

4. Assessing Content Quality and Alignment:

Review the quality and consistency of an influencer's content to ensure it aligns with your brand standards. Analyze the relevance of their content to your target audience, and assess their ability to authentically integrate brand messaging into their content.

5. Examining Influencer Reputation and Credibility:

Research an influencer's reputation and credibility within their niche. Look for signs of expertise, industry recognition, collaborations with reputable brands, and positive sentiment among their followers. A strong and respected influencer adds credibility to your brand.

6. Engaging with Influencers:

Once you've identified potential influencers, it's time to engage with them. Consider these best practices:

- Authentic Outreach: Personalize your initial outreach to demonstrate genuine interest in their content and establish a meaningful connection.

- Offer Value: Provide influencers with incentives or value-added benefits that resonate with their interests, such as exclusive content, early access to products, or collaboration opportunities.

- Collaborative Content Creation: Involve influencers in the creative process to leverage their expertise and ensure their content resonates with their audience while aligning with your brand messaging.

- Build Relationships: Nurture relationships with influencers beyond one-off collaborations. Regularly engage with their content, provide feedback, and maintain open communication channels to foster long-term partnerships.

- Leverage User-Generated Content (UGC): Encourage influencers to create UGC related to your brand or products, which can help amplify your reach and engage their audience.

7. Establishing Clear Expectations:

Clearly communicate your expectations, campaign goals, and deliverables to influencers. Establish guidelines for content creation, disclosure requirements, and brand messaging to ensure alignment and avoid any misunderstandings.

8. Measuring and Evaluating Influencer Campaigns:

Define key performance indicators (KPIs) aligned with your campaign goals, such as reach, engagement, conversions, or sentiment analysis. Utilize analytics tools and track the identified metrics to evaluate the effectiveness of influencer collaborations.

9. Building Long-Term Relationships:

Long-term relationships with influencers can yield more significant benefits. Continuously nurture these relationships, provide ongoing support, and explore opportunities for extended collaborations and ambassador programs.

10. Staying Compliant and Ethical:

Maintain compliance with advertising regulations and ethical guidelines. Ensure that influencers adhere to disclosure requirements for sponsored content and maintain transparency with their audience.

Conclusion:

Identifying and engaging with influencers is a critical component of successful influencer marketing campaigns. By defining your influencer criteria, conducting thorough research, evaluating reach and engagement, assessing content quality and alignment, and examining reputation and credibility, you can identify the right influencers for your brand. Engaging with influencers authentically, establishing clear expectations, measuring campaign effectiveness, and nurturing long-term relationships are key to building successful partnerships. Remember to stay compliant with regulations and ethical guidelines throughout the process. By implementing these strategies and best practices, brands can harness the power of influencers to effectively reach their target audience, build brand awareness, and drive desired actions. Embrace the potential of influencer marketing, and cultivate meaningful connections with influential individuals who can amplify your brand's message and create lasting impact.

8.3 Negotiating and Managing Influencer Partnerships

Mastering Influencer Partnerships: Strategies for Negotiating and Managing Successful Collaborations

Introduction:

Influencer partnerships have become integral to effective marketing strategies, enabling brands to leverage the influence and reach of individuals to engage with their target audience. However, the success of these partnerships relies heavily on the negotiation and management process. In this article, we will explore essential strategies for negotiating influencer partnerships, discuss key aspects to consider during the negotiation phase, and highlight best practices for managing these collaborations to achieve mutual goals and maximize return on investment.

1. Preparing for Negotiations:

Before entering into influencer partnerships, it's crucial to conduct thorough preparation. This includes defining campaign objectives, establishing budgetary constraints, identifying desired deliverables, and researching the influencer's past partnerships to inform your negotiation strategy.

2. Identifying Value Exchanges:

When negotiating with influencers, it's essential to identify mutually beneficial value exchanges. This could involve offering monetary compensation, providing free products or services, offering unique experiences, or granting access to exclusive events or content.

3. Crafting Persuasive Proposals:

Present influencers with compelling proposals that outline the benefits of collaborating with your brand. Highlight the alignment between the influencer's content and your brand values, articulate the campaign's objectives, and clearly define the deliverables and expectations.

4. Navigating Pricing and Compensation:

Determining fair compensation can be a complex process. Consider factors such as the influencer's reach, engagement rates, content quality, industry expertise, and the level of exclusivity desired. Research industry benchmarks and negotiate based on the value the influencer brings to your brand.

5. Outlining Deliverables and Timelines:

Clearly define the scope of work, deliverables, and expected timelines to avoid any miscommunication or misunderstandings. Ensure that both parties have a shared understanding of the content requirements, key messages, and posting schedules.

6. Establishing Content Guidelines:

Provide influencers with detailed content guidelines that align with your brand's aesthetic, messaging, and values. This includes specifications for captions, visual elements, hashtags, and disclosure requirements to maintain brand consistency and legal compliance.

7. Maintaining Communication Channels:

Open and regular communication is vital throughout the partnership. Establish communication channels for feedback, updates, and revisions. Encourage influencers to provide their input and collaborate in refining the content to ensure it resonates with their audience.

8. Reviewing and Approving Content:

Implement a review and approval process to ensure that the content meets your brand's standards and aligns with the agreed-upon guidelines. Promptly provide feedback and approvals to maintain project timelines.

9. Encouraging Authenticity and Creativity:

While maintaining brand guidelines, allow influencers the creative freedom to produce authentic and engaging content that resonates with their audience. Trust their expertise and respect their unique style and storytelling abilities.

10. Monitoring and Measuring Performance:

Continuously monitor the performance of influencer partnerships using relevant metrics such as reach, engagement, conversions, and sentiment analysis. Track the success of the campaign against the defined objectives and make data-driven adjustments as needed.

11. Providing Post-Campaign Follow-Up:

After the campaign concludes, provide influencers with feedback and performance reports. Express gratitude for their collaboration and evaluate the potential for future partnerships. Maintain relationships with influencers for potential ongoing collaborations.

Conclusion:

Negotiating and managing influencer partnerships require careful planning, effective communication, and a mutually beneficial approach. By preparing for negotiations, identifying value exchanges, crafting persuasive proposals, and navigating pricing and compensation discussions, brands can establish successful partnerships with influencers. Additionally, outlining clear deliverables, content guidelines, and communication channels ensures smooth collaboration. Monitoring performance, providing feedback, and fostering ongoing relationships contribute to long-term success. Influencer partnerships offer valuable opportunities to connect with target audiences authentically and drive meaningful engagement. By employing these strategies and best practices, brands can navigate the intricacies of influencer negotiations and management, leading to fruitful collaborations that benefit both the brand and the influencer. Embrace the potential of influencer partnerships and cultivate successful relationships to amplify your brand's reach and influence in the digital landscape.

8.4 Measuring Influencer Marketing ROI

Unveiling the Metrics: Measuring Influencer Marketing ROI for Effective Campaign Evaluation

Introduction:

Influencer marketing has emerged as a powerful strategy for brands to engage their target audience and drive business results. To ensure the success and effectiveness of influencer marketing campaigns, it is crucial to measure the return on investment (ROI) accurately. In this article, we will delve into the importance of measuring influencer marketing ROI, discuss key metrics and strategies for evaluation, and highlight best practices for effectively measuring the impact of influencer partnerships on business objectives.

1. Understanding Influencer Marketing ROI:

Influencer marketing ROI refers to the measurement of the value generated from influencer collaborations in relation to the investment made. It helps brands determine the effectiveness and impact of their influencer marketing campaigns in achieving specific business goals.

2. Defining Campaign Objectives and Key Performance Indicators (KPIs):

Before measuring ROI, it is essential to define clear campaign objectives and establish relevant KPIs. These objectives could include brand awareness, engagement, website traffic, lead generation, sales, or customer retention. Aligning KPIs with business goals is crucial for accurate ROI assessment.

3. Quantitative Metrics for ROI Measurement:

a. Reach and Impressions: Measure the number of people exposed to the influencer content and the total impressions generated.
b. Engagement: Assess the level of audience interaction with the content, including likes, comments, shares, and saves.
c. Website Traffic: Track the number of visitors driven to the website through influencer referrals.
d. Conversions: Measure the number of desired actions taken, such as purchases, sign-ups, or downloads, directly attributed to influencer campaigns.

4. Qualitative Metrics for ROI Measurement:

a. Brand Sentiment: Monitor the sentiment surrounding the brand, including the quality of audience conversations and feedback generated by the influencer campaign.
b. Content Quality and Alignment: Evaluate how well the influencer content aligns with the brand's values, messaging, and aesthetics.
c. Influencer-Generated Content Value: Assess the impact of the influencer's content on the overall perception of the brand and its storytelling capabilities.

5. Tracking and Attribution:

a. UTM Parameters: Utilize unique tracking codes (UTM parameters) to attribute website traffic and conversions directly to influencer campaigns.
b. Affiliate Links: Use affiliate tracking links to attribute sales and conversions generated by influencers.
c. Custom Promo Codes: Assign custom promo codes to influencers to track the number of sales or sign-ups generated by their audience.

6. Calculating Influencer Marketing ROI:

To calculate influencer marketing ROI, compare the total revenue or value generated from the campaign against the total investment. The investment includes costs associated with influencer partnerships, content creation, tracking tools, and other campaign expenses. ROI can be calculated using the formula: (Revenue Generated - Investment) / Investment * 100.

7. Assessing Incremental Lift:

To gauge the incremental impact of influencer marketing, compare the performance during the campaign period with a baseline period. Analyze the lift in key metrics, such as website traffic, engagement, or conversions, to understand the added value delivered by influencer collaborations.

8. Measuring Long-Term Brand Impact:

Influencer marketing can have long-term brand impact beyond immediate ROI. Evaluate factors such as brand awareness, audience growth, customer loyalty, and brand sentiment to assess the lasting effects of influencer campaigns.

9. Best Practices for ROI Measurement:

a. Set Clear Objectives: Clearly define campaign goals and align them with business objectives to guide ROI measurement.
b. Establish Benchmarks: Establish baseline metrics or industry benchmarks to evaluate the effectiveness and impact of influencer campaigns.
c. Implement Advanced Tracking Tools: Utilize tools like Google Analytics, affiliate marketing platforms, and social media analytics to track and attribute results accurately.
d. Evaluate Influencer Fit: Assess the suitability of influencers for your brand by analyzing their audience demographics, engagement rates, and relevance to your target market.
e. Regular Monitoring and Reporting: Continuously monitor campaign performance, measure ROI at regular intervals, and create comprehensive reports to track progress and make data-driven decisions.

Conclusion:

Measuring influencer marketing ROI is critical for brands to assess the effectiveness and impact of their campaigns. By defining clear objectives, identifying relevant KPIs, utilizing quantitative and qualitative metrics, tracking and attributing results, and calculating ROI accurately, brands can gain valuable insights into the value generated from influencer collaborations. It is essential to go beyond immediate revenue and consider long-term brand impact and incremental lift when evaluating ROI. By implementing best practices, continuously monitoring results, and making data-driven optimizations, brands can maximize the effectiveness of influencer marketing, optimize their campaigns, and drive better business outcomes. Embrace the measurement of influencer marketing ROI as a strategic tool to evaluate the success of your campaigns, inform future decision-making, and achieve meaningful results in the dynamic world of influencer marketing.

8.5 Influencer Marketing Best Practices

Mastering Influencer Marketing: 10 Best Practices for Effective Influencer Collaborations

Introduction:

Influencer marketing has revolutionized the way brands connect with their target audience. However, executing successful influencer campaigns requires a strategic and thoughtful approach. In this article, we will delve into the best practices that can help brands optimize their influencer collaborations and drive maximum results. From identifying the right influencers to maintaining authentic relationships, these best practices will ensure a successful influencer marketing journey.

1. Define Clear Campaign Objectives:

Before embarking on an influencer campaign, clearly define your campaign objectives. Determine whether you aim to increase brand awareness, drive sales, boost engagement, or launch a new product. Defining objectives helps shape your influencer selection, messaging, and overall campaign strategy.

2. Thoroughly Research Influencers:

Conduct thorough research to identify influencers who align with your brand values, target audience, and campaign goals. Analyze their content, engagement rates, audience demographics, and authenticity. Look for influencers who have built genuine connections with their followers and possess expertise in your industry or niche.

3. Authenticity and Relevance:

Choose influencers whose content and values align with your brand. Authenticity is key to successful influencer collaborations. Ensure the influencer's voice and style resonate with your target audience. By partnering with influencers who genuinely believe in your brand, you can build credibility and trust among their followers.

4. Develop a Personalized Approach:

When reaching out to influencers, tailor your communication and proposals to each individual. Personalize your messages, demonstrate knowledge of their content, and highlight how your brand collaboration aligns with their interests and audience. A personalized approach shows that you value the influencer's work and increases the likelihood of a positive response.

5. Establish Clear Expectations:

Set clear expectations for deliverables, timelines, and campaign guidelines. Clearly communicate the scope of work, content requirements, brand messaging, and any legal or disclosure obligations. Transparency and clarity in expectations ensure a smooth and productive collaboration.

6. Collaborate on Content Creation:

Involve influencers in the content creation process to leverage their expertise and creative input. Encourage them to infuse their unique style into the content while aligning with your brand guidelines. Co-creation allows for an authentic and engaging content that resonates with both the influencer's audience and your brand.

7. Foster Authentic Relationships:

Nurture authentic relationships with influencers beyond one-off collaborations. Engage with their content, provide support, and show genuine interest in their work. Building long-term relationships with influencers helps establish trust, enables ongoing collaborations, and strengthens brand advocacy.

8. Encourage Disclosure and Transparency:

Promote ethical practices by ensuring influencers disclose sponsored content according to relevant regulations. Encourage them to be transparent with their audience about brand partnerships. Disclosure maintains trust and helps influencers maintain authenticity and credibility.

9. Track and Measure Performance:

Utilize analytics tools and track relevant metrics to measure the performance of influencer campaigns. Monitor reach, engagement, website traffic, conversions, and sentiment analysis. Evaluate the effectiveness of campaigns against defined KPIs to gain insights and optimize future strategies.

10. Analyze and Learn from Results:

Regularly analyze campaign results and learn from the data. Identify what worked well and areas for improvement. Adjust your influencer selection, messaging, or content strategy based on insights gained from campaign performance. Continuously iterate and optimize to achieve better results with each campaign.

Conclusion:

Influencer marketing is a powerful strategy that allows brands to connect with their target audience authentically. By following these best practices, brands can maximize the impact of their influencer collaborations. Defining clear objectives, conducting thorough research, fostering authenticity, developing personalized approaches, and maintaining transparent relationships with influencers are key pillars of successful influencer marketing. By tracking performance, analyzing results, and continuously learning and refining strategies, brands can leverage the power of influencers to drive brand awareness, engagement, and conversions. Embrace these best practices to create impactful and meaningful influencer campaigns that yield long-term success.

9. Mobile Marketing

Mobile marketing: Reaching and engaging mobile users through apps, websites, SMS, or location-based services to boost brand awareness, acquire customers, and drive engagement.

9.1 Mobile Marketing Landscape

Navigating the Mobile Marketing Landscape: Harnessing the Power of Mobile for Effective Campaigns

Introduction:

In today's digital era, mobile devices have become an integral part of our daily lives. As a result, mobile marketing has emerged as a dynamic and powerful strategy for brands to connect with their target audience. In this article, we will explore the mobile marketing landscape, discuss the significance of mobile marketing in today's digital landscape, highlight key mobile marketing channels and strategies, and provide insights into leveraging the power of mobile to drive effective campaigns.

1. The Significance of Mobile Marketing:

Mobile marketing has gained immense significance due to the following factors:
- Mobile Device Penetration: The widespread adoption of smartphones and tablets has led to a massive audience accessible through mobile marketing channels.
- Changing Consumer Behavior: Consumers are increasingly relying on mobile devices for various activities, including internet browsing, shopping, social media, and content consumption.

- Always-Connected Culture: Mobile devices have created an "always-connected" culture, allowing brands to engage with consumers at any time and in any location.
- Personalized and Targeted Marketing: Mobile marketing enables brands to deliver personalized and targeted content, leveraging data such as location, preferences, and browsing history.
- Mobile Advertising Opportunities: Mobile platforms provide diverse advertising options, including in-app ads, mobile websites, mobile search, and push notifications.

2. Mobile Marketing Channels:

a. Mobile Applications (Apps): Brands can develop mobile apps to provide value, engage users, and drive conversions. Apps allow for personalized experiences and push notifications to reach users directly.
b. Mobile-Optimized Websites: Optimizing websites for mobile devices ensures a seamless browsing experience and accessibility across various screen sizes.
c. SMS and MMS Marketing: Brands can utilize SMS (short message service) and MMS (multimedia messaging service) to deliver targeted messages, promotions, or alerts to users' mobile phones.
d. Mobile Search Advertising: Mobile search ads enable brands to target users searching for specific products or services on search engines through their mobile devices.
e. Location-Based Marketing: Leveraging geolocation data, brands can deliver targeted offers, promotions, or content based on users' real-time location.
f. In-App Advertising: Advertising within mobile applications allows brands to reach users while they are engaged with specific apps, providing opportunities for targeted messaging.

3. Mobile Marketing Strategies:

a. Responsive Design: Implementing responsive web design ensures that websites adapt to various screen sizes, providing an optimized user experience across mobile devices.
b. Mobile SEO: Optimizing websites for mobile search enhances visibility and organic search rankings on search engine result pages.
c. App Store Optimization (ASO): Optimizing mobile app listings with relevant keywords, compelling descriptions, and engaging visuals improves discoverability and app store rankings.

d. Push Notifications: Engaging users with personalized push notifications can drive app engagement, inform about new products, offer promotions, or deliver important updates.
e. Mobile Advertising Campaigns: Running targeted mobile ad campaigns across various channels helps drive brand awareness, user engagement, and conversions.
f. Mobile Content Marketing: Creating mobile-friendly content such as articles, videos, or interactive experiences optimized for mobile devices enhances engagement and shareability.
g. Mobile Social Media Marketing: Utilizing social media platforms with mobile-centric features allows brands to reach and engage with their target audience effectively.

4. Mobile Analytics and Measurement:

Utilize mobile analytics tools to measure and evaluate the performance of mobile marketing efforts. Key metrics to consider include:
- Mobile App Installs: Measure the number of app downloads and installs to assess campaign effectiveness.
- Engagement Metrics: Track user behavior within mobile apps or websites, including session duration, screen views, and conversion rates.
- Mobile Ad Performance: Analyze metrics such as click-through rates (CTR), impressions, conversions, and return on ad spend (ROAS) to optimize mobile ad campaigns.
- Mobile Conversion Rates: Measure conversion rates for mobile website visitors or app users to evaluate the effectiveness of mobile user experiences.
- Mobile E-commerce Metrics: Analyze mobile-specific metrics like mobile revenue, average order value (AOV), and mobile conversion rates for e-commerce brands.

5. Best Practices for Mobile Marketing:

a. Mobile-First Approach: Prioritize mobile user experience by designing mobile-friendly websites, optimizing content, and creating mobile-centric campaigns.
b. Personalization and Contextual Targeting: Leverage user data to deliver personalized and contextually relevant content, offers, and recommendations.
c. Optimize Page Load Speed: Mobile users expect fast-loading websites and apps. Optimize loading times to provide a seamless user experience.
d. Streamline User Journeys: Simplify navigation and minimize steps to enhance user engagement and drive conversions.

e. A/B Testing: Test and optimize mobile campaigns, landing pages, and app experiences through A/B testing to identify what resonates best with your audience.

f. Compliance and Privacy: Ensure compliance with data privacy regulations, obtain proper consent, and communicate transparently about data collection and usage.

Conclusion:

Mobile marketing has revolutionized the way brands engage with their target audience. By embracing the mobile marketing landscape, utilizing various channels, implementing effective strategies, and measuring performance accurately, brands can optimize their mobile marketing efforts and drive business growth. Mobile devices offer immense opportunities to deliver personalized, targeted, and timely content to users, enhancing brand visibility, engagement, and conversions. By adopting best practices, staying updated with evolving mobile trends, and continuously optimizing mobile campaigns, brands can successfully navigate the mobile marketing landscape and harness the power of mobile to connect with their audience in meaningful and impactful ways. Embrace the mobile-first approach and embrace the potential of mobile marketing to drive success in the ever-expanding mobile ecosystem.

9.2 Mobile Advertising Formats And Platforms

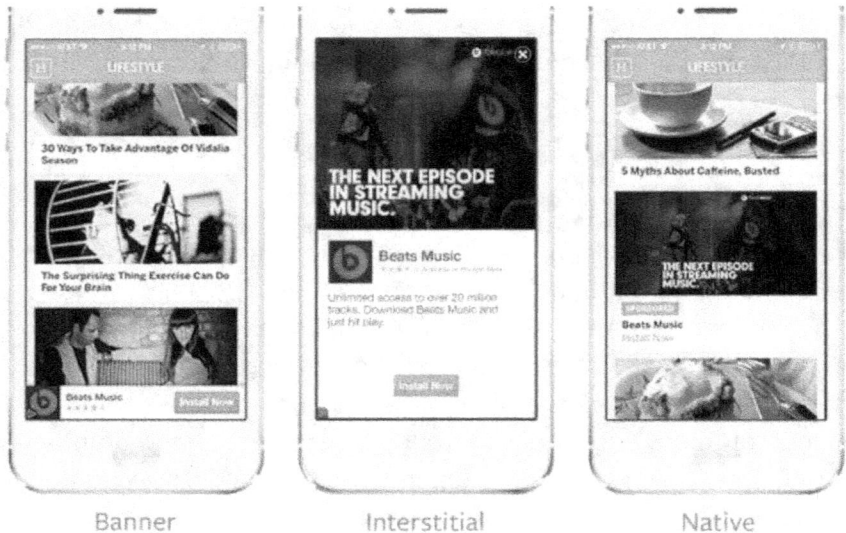

Banner   Interstitial   Native

Exploring Mobile Advertising Formats and Platforms: Maximizing Impact in the Mobile Landscape

Introduction:

In the era of smartphones and tablets, mobile advertising has become an essential component of successful marketing strategies. With a vast user base and diverse engagement opportunities, brands can leverage various mobile advertising formats and platforms to connect with their target audience effectively. In this article, we will explore popular mobile advertising formats, discuss key platforms for mobile advertising, highlight their unique features and advantages, and provide insights into maximizing the impact of mobile advertising campaigns.

1. Mobile Advertising Formats:

a. Banner Ads: Displayed at the top or bottom of a mobile screen, banner ads are static or animated visuals that promote a brand, product, or offer. They are commonly used in mobile apps, mobile websites, and social media platforms.
b. Interstitial Ads: Full-screen ads that appear between app screens or during natural pauses in content consumption. They often include rich media, such as videos or interactive elements, providing engaging experiences.

c. Native Ads: Designed to seamlessly blend with the app or website's content, native ads match the visual style and format of the platform, enhancing user experience and reducing ad disruption.

d. Video Ads: Engaging video content displayed before, during, or after mobile app content, or embedded within mobile websites. Video ads can be short, skippable, or non-skippable, and have proven to be highly effective in capturing user attention.

e. In-App Rewards and Gamified Ads: Offers users incentives, virtual rewards, or game-like experiences in exchange for engaging with ads, enhancing user participation and interaction.

f. App Install Ads: Promote app downloads by featuring an app's key features, benefits, and a direct link to download the app from an app store. Commonly used to drive app installations and user acquisition.

2. Key Mobile Advertising Platforms:

a. Social Media Platforms: Facebook, Instagram, Twitter, and Snapchat offer robust mobile advertising capabilities with highly targeted audience segmentation, precise targeting options, and advanced analytics.

b. Search Engine Advertising: Platforms like Google Ads and Bing Ads provide mobile-specific ad formats and targeting options to reach users actively searching for products or services on their mobile devices.

c. Mobile Ad Networks: These platforms aggregate mobile ad inventory from various publishers and offer a wide reach to advertisers. Examples include Google AdMob, InMobi, and Unity Ads.

d. In-App Advertising Networks: Specifically designed for mobile apps, these networks help advertisers reach users within popular mobile apps across various categories.

e. Mobile DSPs (Demand-Side Platforms): DSPs enable programmatic advertising on mobile devices, allowing advertisers to reach specific audiences through real-time bidding on ad inventory across multiple ad exchanges.

f. Rich Media Ad Platforms: These platforms enable the creation and delivery of interactive and engaging rich media ad formats, such as playable ads, interactive videos, and augmented reality (AR) experiences.

3. Advantages and Considerations:

a. Targeted Reach: Mobile advertising allows brands to target specific demographics, interests, behaviors, and even geographical locations, ensuring messages reach the right audience.

b. Enhanced User Experience: With formats like native ads and interactive rich media, brands can deliver ads that seamlessly integrate into the user experience, reducing ad disruption.
c. Data-Driven Insights: Mobile advertising platforms provide robust analytics and reporting capabilities, allowing advertisers to measure ad performance, user engagement, and conversion tracking.
d. Cross-Device Targeting: Mobile advertising platforms often provide cross-device targeting options, enabling advertisers to reach users across multiple devices, ensuring consistent brand exposure.
e. Responsive Design: Mobile ad formats are designed to be responsive and adapt to various screen sizes and orientations, ensuring optimal user experience on different devices.
f. Ad Blocking Considerations: With the rise of ad-blocking technologies, brands need to consider formats and platforms that are less susceptible to ad-blocking, such as native ads and in-app advertising.

4. Strategies for Effective Mobile Advertising:

a. Target Audience Segmentation: Utilize data-driven insights to identify and segment the target audience based on demographics, interests, behaviors, and contextual relevance.
b. Compelling and Engaging Content: Create visually appealing, concise, and engaging ad content that captures the attention of mobile users and conveys the brand's message effectively.
c. Ad Placement and Frequency: Carefully consider the placement and frequency of ads to ensure they are visible but not intrusive, maintaining a positive user experience.
d. Personalization and Dynamic Creative Optimization: Leverage user data and dynamic creative optimization techniques to deliver personalized and relevant ad experiences based on user preferences and behaviors.
e. Mobile Landing Page Optimization: Ensure mobile landing pages are fast-loading, responsive, and user-friendly to drive conversions and enhance the user experience after ad engagement.
f. Continuous Monitoring and Optimization: Regularly monitor ad performance, analyze data, and optimize campaigns based on insights to maximize ad effectiveness and achieve desired outcomes.
Conclusion:

Mobile advertising formats and platforms offer brands extensive opportunities to connect with their target audience in a highly targeted and engaging manner. By leveraging banner ads, interstitial ads, native ads, video ads, and other formats, brands can captivate mobile users and drive desired actions.

Social media platforms, search engine advertising, mobile ad networks, and programmatic platforms facilitate reaching the right audience at the right time. With enhanced user experiences, precise targeting, robust analytics, and cross-device capabilities, mobile advertising provides a powerful tool for brands to achieve their marketing goals. By considering the advantages and considerations of different mobile advertising formats and platforms, implementing effective strategies, and continuously monitoring and optimizing campaigns, brands can harness the power of mobile advertising and maximize their impact in the ever-evolving mobile landscape.

9.3 App Store Optimization (ASO)

Unlocking Success with App Store Optimization (ASO): Strategies for App Discoverability and User Acquisition

Introduction:

With millions of apps available in app stores, getting your app discovered by users can be a daunting challenge. This is where App Store Optimization (ASO) comes into play. ASO is a crucial process that focuses on optimizing various elements of your app store listing to increase its visibility, improve search rankings, and drive organic downloads. In this article, we will explore the concept of App Store Optimization, discuss its significance in the app marketplace, highlight key ASO strategies, and provide insights on how to effectively optimize your app store presence for maximum app discoverability and user acquisition.

1. Understanding App Store Optimization:

App Store Optimization involves optimizing your app's metadata, visual assets, and other elements to improve its visibility in app store search results and category rankings. ASO encompasses keyword optimization, appealing visual assets, compelling descriptions, positive user ratings, and effective user reviews. ASO helps increase organic downloads, attract engaged users, and boost app revenue.

2. Keyword Research and Optimization:

Performing thorough keyword research is crucial for ASO success. Identify relevant keywords and phrases that users are likely to search for when looking for apps similar to yours. Incorporate these keywords strategically into your app title, subtitle, keyword field, and app description. Balance keyword relevance with natural language and avoid keyword stuffing.

3. Optimizing Visual Assets:

Visual assets play a significant role in attracting potential users. Focus on optimizing your app's icon, screenshots, preview videos, and feature graphics. Create visually appealing and high-quality assets that accurately represent your app's features and benefits. Optimize screenshots to showcase the app's key features and benefits, and use preview videos to provide a glimpse of the app's functionality.

4. Crafting Compelling App Descriptions:

Write clear, concise, and compelling app descriptions that effectively communicate your app's value proposition. Highlight key features, benefits, and unique selling points. Use persuasive language, bullet points, and formatting to enhance readability. Consider localizing your app description for different markets to reach a broader audience.

5. Encouraging Positive User Ratings and Reviews:

Positive ratings and reviews are powerful social proof for potential users. Encourage satisfied users to leave positive reviews by integrating in-app prompts and personalized requests. Respond to user reviews, addressing concerns and providing support. Engage with users to build a positive brand image and encourage word-of-mouth recommendations.

6. Monitoring and Analyzing Performance:

Regularly monitor and analyze key performance metrics related to app downloads, conversion rates, user engagement, and retention. Leverage app store analytics tools and external analytics platforms to gain insights into user behavior, demographic data, and user acquisition channels. Use these insights to make data-driven decisions and iterate on your ASO strategies.

7. A/B Testing and Iterative Optimization:

Conduct A/B tests to compare different variations of your app store elements, such as app icons, screenshots, and app descriptions. Analyze the performance of each variation and iterate based on the results. Continuously refine your ASO strategy by testing and optimizing different elements to enhance app store visibility and conversion rates.

8. Building a Strong App Brand:

Establishing a strong app brand can significantly impact ASO. Create a consistent and recognizable brand identity through your app's name, logo, colors, and visual assets. Develop a compelling value proposition that resonates with your target audience. Build a loyal user base through exceptional user experiences, regular updates, and responsive customer support.

9. Collaborating with Influencers and Partners:

Partnering with influencers and strategic partners can enhance your app's visibility and attract new users. Collaborate with influencers who align with your app's target audience and have a significant following. Encourage them to share their experiences with your app through reviews, testimonials, or sponsored content.

10. Leveraging App Store Advertising:

Consider utilizing app store advertising platforms, such as Apple Search Ads or Google Play Ads, to drive targeted app installs. Optimize your ad campaigns by targeting relevant keywords, refining audience demographics, and monitoring performance. Combine app store advertising with ASO strategies for a comprehensive user acquisition approach.

Conclusion:

App Store Optimization (ASO) is a crucial process for improving the visibility, discoverability, and user acquisition of your mobile app. By strategically optimizing keywords, visual assets, app descriptions, and encouraging positive user ratings and reviews, you can significantly enhance your app's chances of being discovered by potential users. Regular monitoring, analysis, A/B testing, and iterative optimization are essential to refine your ASO strategies and adapt to evolving user preferences. Building a strong app brand, collaborating with influencers, and leveraging app store advertising further contribute to app success. Embrace the power of ASO to stand out in the competitive app marketplace, attract engaged users, and drive organic downloads, ultimately leading to the growth and success of your mobile app.

9.4 SMS Marketing

Unleashing the Power of SMS Marketing: Enhancing Engagement and Driving Results

Introduction:

In today's digital age, SMS (Short Message Service) marketing has emerged as a highly effective and widely adopted strategy for brands to connect with their target audience. With the ubiquity of mobile devices, SMS offers a direct and immediate communication channel that allows brands to reach customers anytime, anywhere. In this article, we will explore the concept of SMS marketing, discuss its significance in the marketing landscape, highlight key benefits, and provide insights on how to effectively leverage SMS to enhance engagement, drive conversions, and build customer relationships.

1. Understanding SMS Marketing:

SMS marketing involves the use of text messages to deliver targeted promotional messages, updates, alerts, or notifications directly to customers' mobile phones. It provides brands with a convenient and highly accessible channel to reach a wide audience instantly.

2. Benefits of SMS Marketing:

a. High Open Rates: SMS boasts exceptionally high open rates, with most messages being read within minutes of delivery. This ensures that your messages have a higher chance of being seen and engaged with by customers.
b. Immediate Reach: SMS offers real-time communication, enabling brands to deliver time-sensitive information, flash sales, limited-time offers, or event reminders instantly.
c. Direct and Personalized Communication: SMS allows for personalized messages that can be tailored to specific customer segments, providing a more personalized and targeted approach.
d. Opt-in and Permission-Based: SMS marketing requires customers to opt-in to receive messages, ensuring that recipients are genuinely interested in your brand and offerings.
e. Cost-Effective: SMS campaigns tend to be more cost-effective than other marketing channels, making it suitable for businesses of all sizes.

3. Types of SMS Marketing Campaigns:

a. Promotional Campaigns: Send SMS messages to promote new products, special offers, discounts, or seasonal sales, generating immediate interest and driving customer action.
b. Transactional Notifications: Provide order confirmations, shipping updates, appointment reminders, or payment notifications to enhance customer experience and ensure seamless communication.
c. Event Invitations and Reminders: Send SMS invitations, RSVP confirmations, and event reminders to boost attendance and engagement for conferences, webinars, or exclusive events.
d. Loyalty Programs: Engage customers through SMS by delivering loyalty rewards, exclusive discounts, or personalized recommendations based on their purchase history or preferences.
e. Feedback and Surveys: Request customer feedback, conduct surveys, or collect testimonials via SMS, allowing customers to provide quick responses and valuable insights.

4. Best Practices for Effective SMS Marketing:

a. Obtain Permission: Ensure compliance with applicable regulations by obtaining explicit permission from customers before sending them SMS messages.
b. Craft Compelling Messages: Keep SMS messages concise, clear, and action-oriented. Use attention-grabbing language, personalized content, and compelling CTAs to drive engagement and conversions.

c. Timing and Frequency: Be mindful of the time zone and preferences of your target audience when scheduling SMS messages. Avoid excessive messaging to prevent customer annoyance or opt-outs.

d. Personalization and Segmentation: Leverage customer data to personalize SMS content and segment your audience based on demographics, purchase history, or behavior, delivering tailored messages that resonate.

e. Provide Opt-Out Options: Include clear instructions on how customers can opt-out of receiving SMS messages, respecting their preferences and complying with regulations.

f. Integrate SMS with Multi-Channel Strategy: Combine SMS with other marketing channels, such as email, social media, or mobile apps, for a cohesive and integrated customer experience.

5. Measurement and Optimization:

a. Track Key Metrics: Monitor key metrics such as delivery rates, open rates, click-through rates (CTRs), and conversion rates to measure the effectiveness of your SMS campaigns.

b. A/B Testing: Conduct A/B tests by sending variations of SMS messages to segments of your audience, allowing you to identify the most effective message content, timing, or CTAs.

c. Analytics and Insights: Leverage SMS analytics tools to gain insights into customer behavior, preferences, and engagement patterns. Use this data to refine your SMS marketing strategies.

d. Continual Improvement: Regularly review and optimize your SMS campaigns based on performance data, customer feedback, and industry trends to maximize results and customer satisfaction.

6. Ensuring Compliance and Building Trust:

a. Comply with Regulations: Familiarize yourself with relevant SMS marketing regulations, such as obtaining opt-in consent and providing clear opt-out options.

b. Data Security and Privacy: Safeguard customer data and ensure secure transmission and storage of information to build trust and maintain customer confidence.

c. Transparency and Clarity: Clearly communicate how customer data will be used and ensure transparency in your SMS marketing practices.

d. Value-Added Content: Provide valuable and relevant content in your SMS messages to enhance customer engagement and foster positive brand interactions.

Conclusion:

SMS marketing offers a powerful and direct communication channel for brands to engage with their audience, drive conversions, and foster customer relationships. By understanding the benefits of SMS marketing, implementing best practices, and continuously optimizing campaigns, brands can unlock the potential of this highly effective marketing strategy. Remember to obtain permission, craft compelling messages, personalize content, and track key metrics to ensure success. SMS marketing, when executed with compliance, respect for customer preferences, and a customer-centric approach, can be a valuable addition to a comprehensive marketing strategy. Embrace the power of SMS marketing to reach customers instantly, deliver timely and personalized messages, and achieve tangible business results.

9.5 Mobile Marketing Analytics

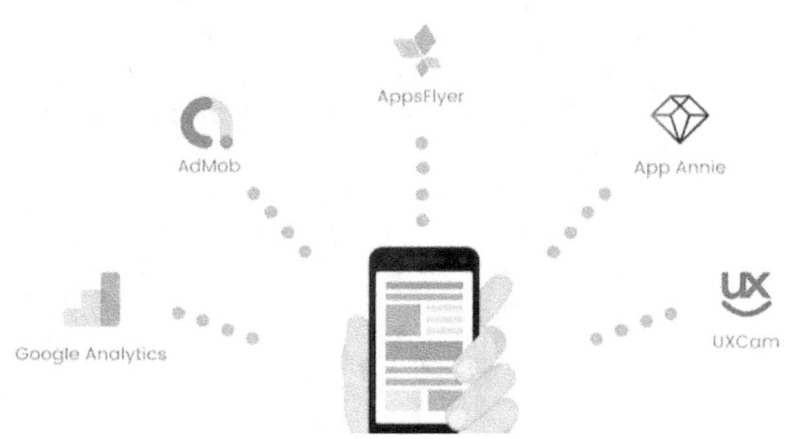

Mobile Marketing Analytics: Unlocking Insights for Optimal Campaign Performance

Introduction:

In the mobile-driven world we live in, effective mobile marketing requires data-driven insights to understand customer behavior, measure campaign performance, and make informed decisions. Mobile marketing analytics plays a crucial role in providing actionable insights to optimize campaigns, improve user experiences, and drive business growth. In this article, we will explore the significance of mobile marketing analytics, discuss key metrics and tools, highlight best practices for mobile analytics implementation, and provide insights on how to leverage analytics to maximize the impact of mobile marketing efforts.

1. The Significance of Mobile Marketing Analytics:

Mobile marketing analytics provides valuable insights into user behavior, engagement, and campaign performance. It helps businesses understand how users interact with mobile apps, websites, and advertising campaigns. Mobile analytics enables brands to measure and track key performance indicators (KPIs), identify trends, make data-driven decisions, and optimize marketing strategies for better outcomes.

2. Key Mobile Marketing Metrics:

a. Acquisition Metrics: Measure user acquisition channels, including app installs, app store page views, and click-through rates (CTRs) for app install ads.
b. Engagement Metrics: Analyze user engagement, including session duration, screen views, bounce rates, and in-app actions, such as clicks, purchases, or form completions.
c. Retention Metrics: Track user retention rates, churn rates, and cohort analysis to understand user loyalty and identify opportunities for retention optimization.
d. Conversion Metrics: Measure conversion rates, revenue per user (RPU), average order value (AOV), and other conversion-related metrics to evaluate campaign effectiveness and revenue generation.
e. Attribution Metrics: Attribute conversions to specific marketing channels or campaigns to understand the impact of various touchpoints in the customer journey.

3. Mobile Analytics Tools:

a. Mobile Analytics Platforms: Robust analytics platforms like Google Analytics for Mobile Apps, Firebase Analytics, and Mixpanel provide comprehensive insights into user behavior, engagement, and conversion metrics.
b. In-App Analytics SDKs: Software Development Kits (SDKs) enable app developers to integrate analytics capabilities directly into their apps, tracking user interactions and events.
c. Attribution Platforms: Attribution platforms like AppsFlyer, Adjust, and Branch help track and attribute conversions to specific marketing campaigns and channels.
d. Heatmaps and User Recording Tools: Tools like Hotjar and Appsee provide visual representations of user interactions, allowing businesses to understand how users navigate and engage with their app or website.

4. Best Practices for Mobile Analytics Implementation:

a. Define Clear Goals and KPIs: Establish specific goals and key performance indicators aligned with your mobile marketing objectives to guide your analytics strategy.

b. Set Up Proper Tracking: Ensure proper implementation of tracking codes, SDKs, and event tracking to capture relevant data points accurately.
c. Segmentation and Cohort Analysis: Segment users based on demographics, behaviors, or user lifecycle stages to gain insights into different user groups and their engagement patterns.
d. Custom Event Tracking: Define and track custom events that are meaningful to your business to capture specific user interactions and actions.
e. A/B Testing: Conduct A/B tests to compare different variations of campaigns, features, or user experiences, allowing you to optimize and improve mobile marketing efforts.
f. Regular Reporting and Analysis: Establish a regular reporting cadence to monitor key metrics, identify trends, and extract actionable insights to drive optimization efforts.

5. Leveraging Mobile Analytics for Optimization:

a. User Journey Analysis: Analyze the user journey from acquisition to conversion, identifying areas of improvement, user drop-off points, and opportunities for optimization.
b. App Store Optimization (ASO): Use mobile analytics to track the impact of ASO efforts on app visibility, downloads, and conversion rates.
c. Conversion Rate Optimization (CRO): Identify bottlenecks or friction points in the conversion funnel and optimize user experiences to improve conversion rates.
d. Personalization and Segmentation: Leverage mobile analytics insights to deliver personalized content, recommendations, and targeted marketing campaigns based on user preferences and behaviors.
e. Attribution Analysis: Analyze the effectiveness of different marketing channels, campaigns, and touchpoints in the user journey to allocate budgets and resources effectively.

6. Privacy and Data Security Considerations:

a. Data Privacy Compliance: Comply with data privacy regulations, such as the General Data Protection Regulation (GDPR), ensuring proper consent and protection of user data.
b. Data Anonymization: Anonymize user data to protect individual privacy while still deriving insights and aggregating data for analysis.
c. Transparent Data Practices: Communicate transparently with users about data collection, usage, and sharing practices, building trust and maintaining user confidence.

Conclusion:

Mobile marketing analytics is essential for businesses to understand user behavior, optimize campaigns, and drive results in the mobile-centric landscape. By measuring and analyzing key mobile marketing metrics, leveraging the right analytics tools, and implementing best practices, brands can unlock valuable insights to inform strategic decisions and improve user experiences. Mobile analytics allows businesses to track acquisition, engagement, retention, and conversion metrics, enabling data-driven optimization and personalized marketing efforts. However, it is crucial to prioritize user privacy and data security, complying with relevant regulations and implementing transparent data practices. Embrace the power of mobile marketing analytics to gain a competitive edge, drive performance, and deliver exceptional experiences that resonate with your mobile audience.

10. Analytics and Reporting

Analytics and reporting: Using data analysis to gain insights into marketing performance, consumer behavior, and campaign effectiveness for data-driven decision-making and optimizing strategies.

10.1 Introduction To Digital Marketing Analytics

Unveiling the Power of Digital Marketing Analytics: Driving Data-Driven Decisions for Success

Introduction:

In the ever-evolving digital landscape, data has become the cornerstone of effective marketing strategies. Digital marketing analytics plays a pivotal role in providing valuable insights into customer behavior, campaign performance, and overall marketing success. By harnessing the power of digital marketing analytics, businesses can make data-driven decisions, optimize their marketing efforts, and drive impactful results. In this article, we will explore the significance of digital marketing analytics, highlight key metrics and tools, discuss the benefits of data-driven decision-making, and provide insights on how to leverage digital marketing analytics to maximize the impact of your marketing campaigns.

1. The Significance of Digital Marketing Analytics:

Digital marketing analytics is the process of collecting, measuring, analyzing, and interpreting data from various digital marketing channels to gain insights into the performance, effectiveness, and impact of marketing efforts. It enables businesses to understand customer behavior, track key performance indicators (KPIs), measure the ROI of marketing campaigns, and identify areas for improvement and optimization.

2. Key Digital Marketing Metrics:

a. Website Traffic and Engagement Metrics: Measure website traffic, page views, bounce rates, time spent on site, and conversion rates to evaluate the effectiveness of your website and user engagement.
b. Email Marketing Metrics: Analyze open rates, click-through rates (CTRs), conversion rates, and unsubscribe rates to assess the performance of email campaigns and optimize email marketing strategies.
c. Social Media Metrics: Track engagement metrics such as likes, shares, comments, and follower growth to gauge the effectiveness of social media campaigns and understand audience engagement.
d. Search Engine Optimization (SEO) Metrics: Measure organic search traffic, keyword rankings, backlinks, and on-page optimization metrics to evaluate the performance of your SEO efforts.
e. Pay-Per-Click (PPC) Metrics: Analyze metrics like click-through rates (CTRs), cost per click (CPC), conversion rates, and return on ad spend (ROAS) to evaluate the effectiveness of PPC campaigns.

3. Digital Marketing Analytics Tools:

a. Google Analytics: A widely used web analytics tool that provides comprehensive insights into website traffic, user behavior, and conversion tracking.
b. Social Media Analytics Platforms: Platforms like Facebook Insights, Twitter Analytics, and LinkedIn Analytics offer detailed metrics and insights into social media performance.
c. Email Marketing Analytics Tools: Email marketing platforms such as Mailchimp and Constant Contact provide analytics features to track email campaign performance and engagement.
d. SEO Analytics Tools: Tools like Google Search Console, SEMrush, and Moz provide data on keyword rankings, organic traffic, and backlink profiles to assess SEO performance.
e. Marketing Automation Platforms: Comprehensive marketing automation platforms like HubSpot and Marketo offer built-in analytics capabilities to track and measure the effectiveness of multi-channel marketing efforts.

4. Benefits of Data-Driven Decision-Making:

a. Improved Campaign Performance: Data-driven decision-making enables marketers to optimize campaigns based on insights and metrics, resulting in improved targeting, engagement, and conversion rates.
b. Enhanced Customer Experience: By understanding customer behavior and preferences through analytics, businesses can deliver personalized and tailored experiences, increasing customer satisfaction and loyalty.
c. Cost Efficiency: Analytics helps identify marketing tactics and channels that deliver the best ROI, allowing businesses to allocate their resources and budgets more effectively.
d. Real-Time Insights: Digital marketing analytics provides real-time data, allowing marketers to monitor campaigns, make adjustments on the fly, and respond quickly to market changes.
e. Competitive Advantage: By leveraging analytics, businesses can gain a competitive edge by staying ahead of industry trends, understanding their target audience better, and delivering more impactful marketing campaigns.

5. Leveraging Digital Marketing Analytics for Success:

a. Define Clear Objectives and KPIs: Establish clear marketing objectives and define key performance indicators that align with your business goals to guide your analytics strategy.
b. Track and Analyze Relevant Metrics: Identify the most relevant metrics for your marketing channels and regularly track and analyze them to measure campaign performance and identify areas for improvement.
c. Segment and Target Audience: Leverage analytics to segment your audience based on demographics, behaviors, and preferences, allowing for more personalized and targeted marketing campaigns.
d. A/B Testing and Optimization: Conduct A/B tests to compare different variations of campaigns, landing pages, or messaging, and use analytics to analyze results and optimize your marketing efforts.
e. Data Integration and Insights: Integrate data from various marketing channels to gain a holistic view of your marketing performance, allowing you to uncover valuable insights and make informed decisions.

6. Privacy and Data Security Considerations:

a. Compliance with Data Privacy Regulations: Ensure compliance with data privacy regulations such as the General Data Protection Regulation (GDPR) and the California Consumer Privacy Act (CCPA) to protect customer data and maintain trust.

b. Anonymization and Data Protection: Implement data anonymization techniques and robust data security measures to protect customer information and maintain data integrity.

c. Transparent Data Practices: Communicate transparently with customers about data collection, usage, and sharing practices, ensuring they understand how their data is being utilized.

Conclusion:

Digital marketing analytics is a powerful tool that empowers businesses to unlock insights, make data-driven decisions, and optimize their marketing efforts. By tracking and analyzing key metrics, leveraging analytics tools, and adopting a data-driven approach, businesses can gain a competitive advantage, enhance customer experiences, and achieve marketing success. Embrace the power of digital marketing analytics to understand customer behavior, measure campaign performance, and optimize marketing strategies for optimal results in the ever-evolving digital landscape.

10.2 Setting Key Performance Indicators (KPIs)

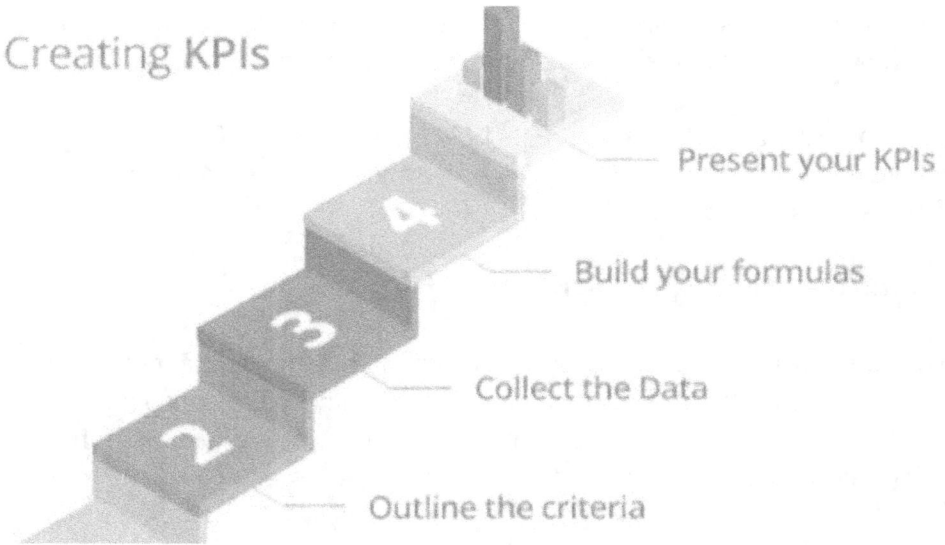

Setting Key Performance Indicators (KPIs): Defining Metrics for Measuring Success

Introduction:

In today's data-driven business landscape, setting Key Performance Indicators (KPIs) is essential for measuring progress, evaluating performance, and achieving organizational goals. KPIs are quantifiable metrics that provide valuable insights into the effectiveness and success of strategies, projects, and initiatives. By setting clear and relevant KPIs, businesses can align their efforts, track progress, and make data-driven decisions to drive success. In this article, we will explore the importance of setting KPIs, discuss the characteristics of effective KPIs, highlight key considerations in setting KPIs, and provide insights on how to define and measure KPIs for different business functions.

1. The Importance of Setting KPIs:

Setting KPIs is crucial for several reasons:
a. Goal Alignment: KPIs ensure that all stakeholders are aligned with the organization's strategic objectives and working towards the same goals.

b. Performance Evaluation: KPIs provide a clear framework for evaluating performance, allowing businesses to assess progress and identify areas for improvement.

c. Data-Driven Decision-Making: KPIs provide measurable data and insights that enable informed decision-making and help prioritize resources and efforts.

d. Accountability and Motivation: KPIs hold individuals and teams accountable for their performance, foster a sense of ownership, and motivate employees to strive for excellence.

2. Characteristics of Effective KPIs:

a. Relevance: KPIs should directly align with the business objectives and reflect the critical aspects of performance that contribute to success.

b. Measurability: KPIs should be quantifiable and objectively measurable, allowing for accurate tracking and comparison over time.

c. Specificity: KPIs should be specific and well-defined, focusing on a particular aspect of performance rather than general indicators.

d. Realistic and Attainable: KPIs should be challenging yet attainable within the given time frame and resources.

e. Time-Bound: KPIs should have a defined time frame for achievement, enabling regular assessment and adjustment of strategies.

3. Considerations in Setting KPIs:

a. Business Objectives: KPIs should directly contribute to the overarching goals of the organization and align with its mission and vision.

b. Data Availability: Consider the availability and accessibility of data required to measure the selected KPIs effectively.

c. Industry Benchmarks: Research industry benchmarks and standards to ensure KPIs are set at a level that reflects competitive performance.

d. Balance: Ensure a balance between leading indicators (predictive metrics) and lagging indicators (outcome-based metrics) to provide a comprehensive view of performance.

e. Stakeholder Alignment: Engage key stakeholders in the KPI-setting process to ensure their buy-in and alignment with organizational goals.

4. Setting KPIs for Different Business Functions:

a. Marketing: KPIs could include metrics like conversion rates, customer acquisition costs, website traffic, lead generation, and social media engagement.

b. Sales: KPIs may include metrics such as sales revenue, customer retention rates, conversion rates, average deal size, and sales cycle length.
c. Customer Service: KPIs could encompass metrics like customer satisfaction scores, average response time, first-call resolution rates, and customer retention rates.
d. Finance: KPIs may include metrics such as revenue growth, profitability ratios, return on investment (ROI), and cash flow management.
e. Operations: KPIs could encompass metrics like production efficiency, on-time delivery, quality control measures, and inventory turnover ratios.

5. Defining and Measuring KPIs:

a. Clearly Define KPIs: Each KPI should have a clear definition, including the measurement unit, calculation methodology, and desired target.
b. Establish Data Collection Mechanisms: Determine the data sources, systems, and tools required to collect and analyze relevant data for measuring the KPIs.
c. Set Baselines and Targets: Establish baselines to understand the current performance level and set realistic targets for improvement.
d. Regularly Monitor and Review KPIs: Continuously track and analyze the performance against established KPIs, using real-time data to evaluate progress.
e. Adjust and Improve: Use KPI insights to identify areas for improvement, make adjustments to strategies, and optimize performance.

6. Communicating and Cascading KPIs:

a. Organizational Alignment: Ensure that KPIs are communicated throughout the organization, cascading from top-level objectives to individual goals, fostering alignment and shared accountability.
b. Transparency and Visibility: Share KPI progress with relevant stakeholders through regular reporting and dashboards, promoting transparency and accountability.
c. Performance Feedback and Recognition: Provide timely feedback and recognition for achieving or exceeding KPI targets, reinforcing a culture of performance and continuous improvement.
d. Performance Reviews: Integrate KPI discussions into performance reviews to assess individual and team contributions to overall organizational goals.
e. Revisit and Revise: Regularly review and revise KPIs as business objectives evolve, market conditions change, or new opportunities arise.

Conclusion:

Setting effective KPIs is vital for organizations to evaluate performance, track progress, and drive success. By defining measurable and relevant KPIs, businesses can align efforts, make data-driven decisions, and optimize strategies across various business functions. It is crucial to consider factors like relevance, measurability, specificity, and time frames when setting KPIs, while also involving key stakeholders in the process. Defining and measuring KPIs require clear definitions, data collection mechanisms, and ongoing monitoring and review. Communicating and cascading KPIs throughout the organization ensures alignment, transparency, and accountability. Regular evaluation, adjustment, and improvement of KPIs are necessary to drive continuous growth and success. Embrace the power of setting KPIs to measure progress, inspire performance, and propel your organization towards its goals.

10.3 Web Analytics Tools (Google Analytics)

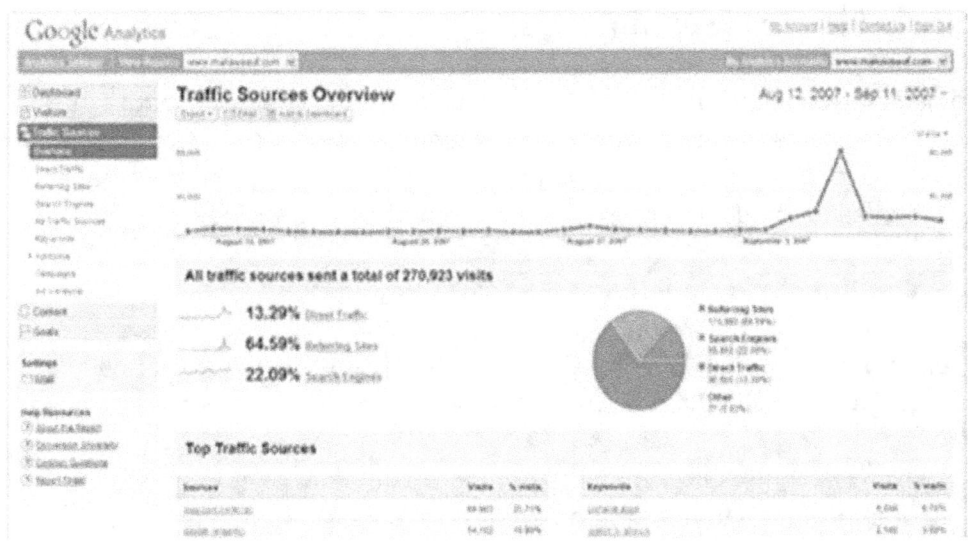

Unleashing the Power of Web Analytics Tools: A Comprehensive Guide to Google Analytics

Introduction:

In today's digital age, understanding user behavior on websites is essential for businesses to optimize their online presence, improve user experiences, and drive measurable results. Web analytics tools provide valuable insights into website traffic, user engagement, conversion rates, and other key performance indicators. Among the top web analytics tools available, Google Analytics stands out as a powerful and widely adopted platform. In this article, we will explore the significance of web analytics, delve into the features and benefits of Google Analytics, highlight key metrics and reports, and provide insights on how to leverage Google Analytics to gain actionable insights and enhance online performance.

1. The Importance of Web Analytics:

Web analytics enables businesses to understand how users interact with their websites, identify strengths and weaknesses, and make data-driven decisions to optimize their online presence. By leveraging web analytics tools, businesses can track website performance, measure marketing campaign effectiveness, improve user experiences, and maximize return on investment.

2. Introduction to Google Analytics:

Google Analytics is a robust web analytics platform offered by Google that provides businesses with comprehensive insights into website traffic, user behavior, and conversion tracking. It offers a range of features, from basic visitor statistics to advanced analysis and reporting capabilities.

3. Key Features and Benefits of Google Analytics:

a. Real-Time Reporting: Monitor website activity in real-time, track active users, page views, and traffic sources, enabling immediate response to user behavior.
b. Audience Insights: Gain valuable demographic data, user interests, and behavior information to understand and target specific audience segments effectively.
c. Acquisition Analysis: Measure the performance of various marketing channels, such as organic search, paid advertising, social media, and referrals, to optimize marketing strategies.
d. Behavior Tracking: Track user interactions, including page views, session durations, bounce rates, and conversion paths, to identify areas for website optimization and improved user experiences.
e. Conversion Tracking: Set up goals and track conversions, such as form submissions, newsletter sign-ups, or e-commerce transactions, to measure the effectiveness of marketing efforts and identify conversion bottlenecks.

4. Key Metrics and Reports in Google Analytics:

a. Audience Metrics: Measure metrics like sessions, users, page views, average session duration, and bounce rates to understand overall website engagement.
b. Acquisition Metrics: Analyze metrics such as traffic sources, referral websites, organic search keywords, and campaign performance to evaluate the effectiveness of marketing channels.
c. Behavior Metrics: Track metrics like page views, exit rates, conversion funnels, and event tracking to gain insights into user behavior and identify areas for optimization.
d. E-commerce Metrics: For e-commerce websites, track metrics such as revenue, average order value, conversion rates, and product performance to assess online sales performance.

e. Custom Reports: Customize reports based on specific business needs, combining various metrics and dimensions to gain deeper insights into website performance.

5. Leveraging Google Analytics for Actionable Insights:

a. Goal Tracking: Set up goals in Google Analytics to measure specific user interactions or conversions, such as form submissions, downloads, or newsletter sign-ups.
b. E-commerce Tracking: Implement e-commerce tracking to gain insights into online sales, revenue, product performance, and customer behavior.
c. Segmentation: Utilize audience segmentation to analyze user behavior based on demographics, geography, device type, or marketing channels, enabling more targeted and personalized marketing strategies.
d. Conversion Funnels: Analyze conversion funnels to identify drop-off points and optimize the user journey for higher conversion rates.
e. A/B Testing: Utilize Google Analytics to track and compare the performance of different variations of website pages, content, or marketing campaigns, allowing data-driven decision-making for optimization.
f. Custom Alerts: Set up custom alerts to receive notifications for significant changes in website metrics, helping to identify and address issues promptly.

6. Advanced Features and Integrations:

a. Google Tag Manager: Integrate Google Analytics with Google Tag Manager to simplify tracking code implementation and manage tags for marketing and analytics tools.
b. Enhanced E-commerce Tracking: Implement enhanced e-commerce tracking to gain deeper insights into online sales performance, product merchandising, and customer behavior.
c. Custom Dimensions and Metrics: Extend Google Analytics with custom dimensions and metrics to track specific user interactions, behaviors, or business-specific data.
d. Data Import: Import offline data, such as CRM data or point-of-sale data, into Google Analytics for a more comprehensive view of customer interactions and attribution analysis.
e. Google Analytics API: Leverage the Google Analytics API to extract data programmatically, build custom dashboards, and integrate analytics data with other business systems.

7. Privacy and Data Security Considerations:

a. Data Privacy Compliance: Ensure compliance with data privacy regulations, such as the General Data Protection Regulation (GDPR), by anonymizing IP addresses, providing clear privacy policies, and obtaining necessary user consent.

b. Data Retention Settings: Configure data retention settings in Google Analytics to align with your organization's data retention policies and compliance requirements.

c. User and Account Access Control: Set up appropriate user roles and permissions to ensure that access to Google Analytics data is granted only to authorized individuals.

d. Data Sharing and Third-Party Integrations: Review and manage data sharing settings with third-party applications and platforms, ensuring alignment with your privacy preferences and compliance standards.

Conclusion:

Google Analytics is a powerful web analytics tool that empowers businesses to gain deep insights into website performance, user behavior, and marketing campaign effectiveness. By leveraging the features and capabilities of Google Analytics, businesses can optimize their online presence, improve user experiences, and drive measurable results. With a wide range of metrics, reports, and customization options, Google Analytics offers a comprehensive solution for businesses seeking actionable insights to inform their marketing strategies. It is essential to consider privacy and data security considerations while implementing and utilizing Google Analytics to ensure compliance with regulations and maintain user trust. Embrace the power of Google Analytics to unlock the potential of your website, enhance user experiences, and drive online success in the dynamic digital landscape.

10.4 Data Analysis And Interpretation

Mastering Data Analysis and Interpretation: Unlocking Insights for Informed Decision-Making

Introduction:

In today's data-driven world, organizations have access to vast amounts of data that can provide valuable insights and drive informed decision-making. However, the true value lies in the ability to analyze and interpret data effectively. Data analysis and interpretation involve examining data sets, uncovering patterns, trends, and correlations, and deriving meaningful insights to guide strategic decisions. In this article, we will explore the significance of data analysis and interpretation, discuss key steps and techniques, highlight common challenges, and provide insights on how to master the art of data analysis and interpretation for maximizing business impact.

1. The Significance of Data Analysis and Interpretation:

Data analysis and interpretation are essential for several reasons:
a. Decision-Making: Data analysis helps organizations make informed decisions based on evidence and insights, mitigating risks and improving outcomes.

b. Performance Evaluation: Analyzing data enables organizations to evaluate their performance, identify strengths and weaknesses, and optimize processes for better results.
c. Forecasting and Predictive Analytics: Data analysis allows organizations to predict future trends, anticipate customer behavior, and plan strategies accordingly.
d. Continuous Improvement: By analyzing data, organizations can uncover opportunities for improvement, implement data-driven solutions, and drive continuous growth.

2. Key Steps in Data Analysis and Interpretation:

a. Define Objectives: Clearly define the objectives and questions you want to answer through data analysis to ensure focus and relevance.
b. Data Collection and Preparation: Gather relevant and reliable data, clean and organize it for analysis, ensuring data quality and accuracy.
c. Exploratory Data Analysis: Conduct initial exploratory analysis to understand data distributions, identify outliers, and detect patterns or relationships.
d. Statistical Analysis: Apply statistical techniques to uncover insights, such as hypothesis testing, regression analysis, or clustering, depending on the nature of the data and objectives.
e. Visualization: Utilize visualizations, such as charts, graphs, or dashboards, to present data in a visually appealing and easily understandable format.
f. Interpretation and Insights: Analyze the results, interpret findings in the context of the objectives, and derive actionable insights to guide decision-making.

3. Techniques for Data Analysis and Interpretation:

a. Descriptive Statistics: Summarize and describe data using measures such as mean, median, mode, standard deviation, or frequency distributions.
b. Inferential Statistics: Make inferences or predictions about a population based on a sample, using techniques like hypothesis testing or confidence intervals.
c. Data Mining: Apply advanced algorithms and techniques to uncover patterns, relationships, or anomalies in large datasets.
d. Predictive Analytics: Utilize statistical modeling and machine learning algorithms to predict future outcomes or trends based on historical data.
e. Text Mining and Sentiment Analysis: Analyze text data to extract meaningful insights, sentiments, or trends from customer reviews, social media comments, or survey responses.

4. Common Challenges in Data Analysis and Interpretation:

a. Data Quality and Integrity: Ensuring the accuracy, completeness, and reliability of data can be challenging, requiring proper data collection and cleaning processes.
b. Data Volume and Complexity: Dealing with large datasets or complex data structures may require specialized tools or techniques for efficient analysis.
c. Bias and Interpretation Errors: Avoiding bias in data analysis and interpretation is crucial to ensure accurate and unbiased insights.
d. Lack of Context: Understanding the context of the data and its limitations is essential for proper interpretation and avoiding misinterpretation.
e. Data Privacy and Security: Protecting sensitive data and complying with privacy regulations is crucial throughout the data analysis process.

5. Best Practices for Data Analysis and Interpretation:

a. Clearly Define Objectives: Start with clear objectives and questions to guide the analysis and ensure relevance and focus.
b. Use a Structured Approach: Follow a systematic approach, including defining variables, selecting appropriate analysis techniques, and documenting the process.
c. Cross-Validation and Peer Review: Validate results by cross-referencing with external data sources or involving peers in reviewing the analysis and interpretation.
d. Visualize Data Effectively: Use visualizations to present data in a clear, concise, and visually appealing manner, aiding comprehension and insights.
e. Continuously Learn and Improve: Embrace a learning mindset, update skills, and stay updated with new techniques, tools, and best practices in data analysis.

6. Communication and Actionable Insights:

a. Clear Communication: Communicate findings and insights in a clear and concise manner, tailored to the audience, using visuals and narratives that resonate with stakeholders.
b. Actionable Recommendations: Provide actionable recommendations based on the insights derived from the data analysis, enabling stakeholders to take informed actions.
c. Iterative Process: Data analysis and interpretation should be an iterative process, allowing for feedback, adjustment, and further exploration as new data or questions arise.

d. Collaborative Approach: Foster collaboration between data analysts, domain experts, and decision-makers to ensure a comprehensive understanding of the data and its implications.

Conclusion:

Data analysis and interpretation are critical for organizations to leverage the power of data and drive informed decision-making. By following a structured approach, utilizing appropriate techniques, and embracing best practices, businesses can unlock valuable insights from their data, uncover patterns, make predictions, and optimize processes for success. However, it is crucial to address challenges related to data quality, bias, and privacy to ensure accurate and reliable results. Effective communication of findings and actionable insights is key to driving impact and achieving desired outcomes. Embrace the art of data analysis and interpretation to harness the potential of your data, gain a competitive edge, and propel your organization towards data-driven success.

10.5 Reporting And Performance Optimization

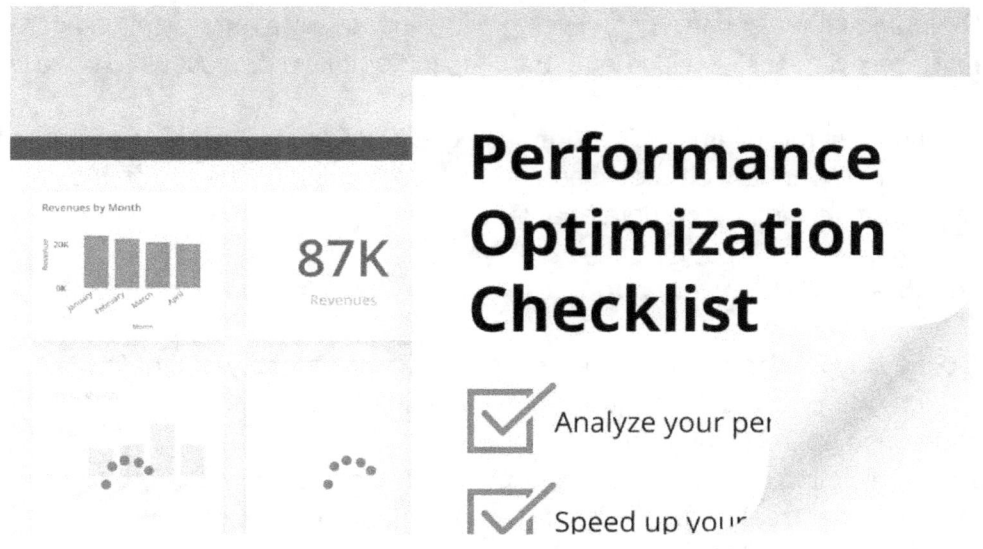

Reporting and Performance Optimization: Maximizing Insights for Data-Driven Decision-Making

Introduction:

In today's data-rich business landscape, reporting and performance optimization are essential components of successful data-driven decision-making. Effective reporting provides organizations with valuable insights into their performance, enabling them to track key metrics, identify trends, and make informed strategic decisions. Performance optimization involves using these insights to identify areas for improvement, implement changes, and drive better outcomes. In this article, we will explore the significance of reporting and performance optimization, discuss key steps and best practices, highlight the benefits of data-driven decision-making, and provide insights on how to leverage reporting and performance optimization to maximize business success.

1. The Importance of Reporting and Performance Optimization:

Reporting and performance optimization offer several benefits:
a. Performance Evaluation: Reporting allows organizations to measure their performance against key metrics, identify successes and areas for improvement, and make data-driven decisions to optimize outcomes.

b. Strategic Alignment: Reporting ensures alignment between organizational goals and performance, providing a clear understanding of progress and areas that require attention.
c. Resource Optimization: By analyzing performance data, organizations can identify inefficiencies, reallocate resources, and optimize processes to drive better results.
d. Continuous Improvement: Performance optimization enables organizations to continuously enhance processes, products, and services based on insights derived from reporting and data analysis.

2. Key Steps in Reporting and Performance Optimization:

a. Define Key Performance Indicators (KPIs): Clearly identify and define KPIs that align with organizational goals, providing a focus for reporting and performance optimization efforts.
b. Data Collection and Analysis: Collect relevant data from various sources, clean and organize it for analysis, and employ appropriate tools and techniques to extract insights.
c. Establish Reporting Framework: Develop a reporting framework that outlines the frequency, format, and audience for reports, ensuring that information is delivered in a timely and digestible manner.
d. Monitor and Track Performance: Regularly track and monitor performance against established KPIs, using visualizations and dashboards to provide a comprehensive view of progress.
e. Analyze Performance Data: Analyze performance data to identify trends, patterns, and areas for improvement, drawing actionable insights that drive performance optimization.
f. Implement Changes and Measure Impact: Based on insights gained from reporting, implement changes and interventions to optimize performance, and measure the impact of these interventions over time.

3. Best Practices for Reporting and Performance Optimization:

a. Define Relevant Metrics: Choose metrics that align with organizational goals and provide actionable insights, ensuring they are measurable, specific, and relevant.
b. Clear and Visual Communication: Use visualizations, charts, and graphs to present data in a clear and easily understandable format, facilitating better comprehension and decision-making.
c. Regular Reporting Cadence: Establish a regular reporting cadence to ensure consistent monitoring of performance and the timely availability of insights for decision-making.

d. Contextualize Data: Provide context and explanations for data trends and anomalies to enhance understanding and guide decision-making processes.

e. Collaborative Approach: Foster collaboration among stakeholders, including data analysts, department heads, and decision-makers, to ensure a shared understanding of reporting findings and drive collective decision-making.

4. Benefits of Data-Driven Decision-Making:

a. Informed Decision-Making: Data-driven decision-making ensures that decisions are based on evidence and insights derived from data analysis, minimizing guesswork and bias.

b. Performance Optimization: By leveraging data insights, organizations can identify opportunities for improvement, implement changes, and optimize processes, leading to enhanced performance and outcomes.

c. Resource Allocation: Data-driven decision-making enables organizations to allocate resources more effectively by identifying high-performing areas and areas that require additional investment or improvement.

d. Agility and Adaptability: Data-driven decision-making empowers organizations to respond quickly to changing market conditions and customer needs, making timely adjustments to strategies and tactics.

e. Competitive Advantage: By utilizing data to make informed decisions, organizations gain a competitive edge by staying ahead of market trends, anticipating customer preferences, and delivering better experiences.

5. Continuous Improvement and Iterative Optimization:

a. Iterative Approach: Reporting and performance optimization should be an ongoing and iterative process, continuously evaluating performance, implementing changes, and measuring impact.

b. Test and Learn: Embrace a test-and-learn mindset by conducting experiments, A/B tests, or pilot programs to gather insights, validate hypotheses, and drive performance optimization.

c. Feedback and Performance Reviews: Incorporate feedback loops and performance reviews to monitor progress, provide constructive feedback, and drive continuous improvement.

d. Benchmarking and Industry Analysis: Compare performance metrics against industry benchmarks and conduct competitive analysis to gain insights and identify areas for improvement.

e. Technology and Automation: Leverage technology and automation tools to streamline data collection, analysis, and reporting processes, allowing for more efficient and effective performance optimization.

6. Actionable Insights and Decision-Making:

a. Translate Insights into Action: Ensure that insights gained from reporting and data analysis are translated into actionable steps and interventions that drive performance improvement.
b. Decision-Making Framework: Establish a decision-making framework that considers both quantitative data and qualitative insights to make well-informed and holistic decisions.
c. Stakeholder Involvement: Involve key stakeholders in the decision-making process, considering their expertise and perspectives to enhance the quality and acceptance of decisions.
d. Monitor and Adjust: Continuously monitor the impact of decisions and interventions, adjusting strategies and tactics as needed to optimize performance.
e. Communication and Alignment: Communicate reporting findings and decision outcomes effectively to stakeholders, ensuring alignment and shared understanding of goals and actions.

Conclusion:

Reporting and performance optimization are integral components of data-driven decision-making, providing organizations with the insights and tools necessary to track progress, identify areas for improvement, and drive optimal performance. By following key steps and best practices, organizations can establish effective reporting frameworks, leverage data insights, and make informed decisions that enhance outcomes and align with strategic objectives. Data-driven decision-making empowers organizations to respond to market dynamics, optimize resource allocation, and gain a competitive edge in an increasingly data-centric business landscape. Embrace the power of reporting and performance optimization to unlock the full potential of your data, drive continuous improvement, and achieve sustained success in today's fast-paced and ever-changing business environment.

www.ingramcontent.com/pod-product-compliance
Lightning Source LLC
Chambersburg PA
CBHW082203220526
45470CB00010B/3029